I REMEMBER
HERMAN
HOEKSEMA

I REMEMBER HERMAN HOEKSEMA

Personal Remembrances of a Great Man

David J. Engelsma

REFORMED
FREE PUBLISHING
ASSOCIATION
Jenison, Michigan

©2020 Reformed Free Publishing Association
2021 Second printing—revised and expanded version

Scripture cited is taken from the King James (Authorized) Version

Reformed Free Publishing Association
1894 Georgetown Center Drive
Jenison, Michigan 49428
616-457-5970
www.rfpa.org
mail@rfpa.org

Cover design by Erika Kiel
Interior design by Katherine Lloyd / theDESKonline.com

ISBN 978-1-944555-76-4
ISBN 978-1-944555-77-1 (ebook)
LCCN 2020951160

Contents

Preface

———

It is my purpose with this short book to relate some of my remembrances of Herman Hoeksema. I do not intend to write a biography. I do not claim that the events I describe were of any special importance for the church. But I do think that these recollections may be of some benefit to the members of the Protestant Reformed Churches, especially the younger members, who never knew the man. The remembrances will show something of the man to those who know Hoeksema only as a theologian and an author.

The occasion for the remembrances is the long span of time between the life of Hoeksema and the majority of members of the Protestant Reformed Churches today. Hoeksema died in 1965, more than fifty years ago. No one under fifty or sixty years of age has any personal recollection of the man. Among the ministers, at the time of this writing I am one of only two men to have had all three years of his seminary training under Herman Hoeksema. Few of the active ministers knew him. The memory of the man fades fast.

The reason for the remembrances is that Herman Hoeksema was a great man. He was a great man of God on behalf of the Protestant Reformed Churches. He was a great man of God for the Reformed faith in the world. He was a great man of God in and for the church of Jesus Christ.

1

Many will dispute this judgment as the biased esteem of a former pupil and ardent, if not blind, disciple. But they will be wrong. For one thing, after fifty-seven years in the ministry, having read widely in the history of the church and of the world, having observed closely events ecclesiastical and civil, having experienced much in the covenant and in society, and having learned to make judgments in light of scripture, the creeds, and the history of the Christian church, I am a blind disciple of no man (if ever I was), including Herman Hoeksema. For another thing, my judgment of Hoeksema's greatness is based on solid, objective, indeed incontrovertible evidence. Christ will display the true greatness of the man—as his own work of grace—in the final judgment, when the last in the judgment of men shall be first by the judgment of God.

—David J. Engelsma

Preface to the Second Printing

———

The reprinting of this work of remembrances of Herman Hoeksema enables me to improve the work both as to form and content.

Regarding the form, there are now chapter headings. There are also corrections of dates and grammatical errors.

The improvements of content are more significant. One is the addition of an incident that demonstrates that, sharp and uncompromising as Hoeksema was in doctrinal controversy, he could be magnanimous in his personal dealings with his theological adversaries. Not all stalwart defenders of the faith share this gift, or even esteem it a gift.

It is cause of gratitude on my part—and surprise—that the first edition of this work has reached a goodly number of ministers and theologians outside the Protestant Reformed Churches, indeed outside the circle of Reformed churches remotely connected with the Protestant Reformed Churches. Some have expressed appreciation that the book has introduced Hoeksema to them. Others have responded that they now see Hoeksema in a different light than before. Brief as it is, at the very beginning of the book, the account of Hoeksema's theology has been helpful to others.

— David J. Engelsma
March, 2021

Chapter 1

THEOLOGIAN
OF SOVEREIGN GRACE

Hoeksema was a great man of God in that he knew, confessed, and taught by word and pen the truth of the word of God as rightly and authoritatively set forth in comprehensive and systematic form in the "Three Forms of Unity." He confessed the truth particularly with regard to its central message: salvation from sin by the sovereign grace of God in Jesus Christ alone.

Even his theological and ecclesiastical foes acknowledged Hoeksema's soundness in the Reformed faith and his unswerving commitment to the gospel of sovereign grace as confessed by the Synod of Dordt in the Canons. When in 1924 the Christian Reformed Church condemned the doctrine that Hoeksema taught, preliminary to deposing him, they themselves testified that he was Reformed in the fundamental truths of the Reformed creeds. Unwittingly, indeed contrary to their intention, they increased their praise of him when they added that he had a tendency towards "onesidedness." For they meant that he was "onesided" in his magnifying of the sovereignty of the grace of God in salvation. What a glorious epitaph!

In a long and frank discussion of Hoeksema and the Dutch Reformed theologian, Klaas Schilder, the doctrines they taught,

Herman Hoeksema while a pastor and writing to the boys fighting in WWII. These letters and responses were published in the *Beacon Lights* magazine.

and the churches they served that I had with Professor J. Douma of the Reformed Churches in the Netherlands ("liberated") in the early 1980s at the Kampen Seminary, Dr. Douma freely acknowledged that a difference between the two theologians was that "your man [Hoeksema] consistently applied predestination—election and reprobation—to the covenant, whereas my man [Schilder] did not." Consistency, particularly regarding divine predestination as source and cause of all salvation, is not a defect in a Reformed theologian.

In his theological memoirs, the famed Dutch Reformed theologian, G. C. Berkouwer, informed the theological world that he deliberately framed his own theology in (an adversary) relation to the theology of Herman Hoeksema. Hoeksema's theology was Berkouwer's foil. Berkouwer went on to assert that Hoeksema developed all his theology in harmony with God's eternal decree of predestination as no other theologian had done.

Whether this is indeed the case may be questioned. Calvin certainly developed his (biblical) theology in basic harmony with predestination, as did others in the Reformed tradition.

Nevertheless, Berkouwer's judgment is the highest praise of Herman Hoeksema, regardless that Berkouwer did not mean it so. It recognized Hoeksema as a great man in the Reformed churches, for whatever theology harmonizes with and extols predestination is the truth, whereas whatever contradicts or obscures predestination is the lie.

Of course, Reformed theologians and churches that shy from "onesidedness" in the direction of honoring God's sovereign grace in salvation, as though this "onesidedness" were the greatest of all doctrinal evils, will understand Berkouwer's judgment as disparagement of Hoeksema. These are the theologians and churches that are "onesided" in the direction of the responsibility of man, not only in that responsibility is their main message, but also because in their sermons and writings "responsibility" challenges, contradicts, and denies divine sovereignty. Such is the popular doctrine of an impotent love of God for all without exception in the preaching of the gospel, a frustrated desire of God to save all by the preaching of the gospel, and a resistible grace that goes out to all men in the preaching of the gospel.

Development of the Truth of Grace

Hoeksema was a great man of God in that the Spirit of Christ used him to develop the gospel of grace. Not all good and faithful ministers of the word also develop the truth. Herman Hoeksema did.

There is development of dogma in the history of the post-apostolic church. This is the work of the Spirit of truth leading the church to an ever richer, deeper, fuller, and purer understanding of the revelation of holy scripture. The Spirit uses theologians for this work. He used Hoeksema.

Hoeksema taught the particularity and sovereignty of God's grace in the preaching of the gospel. Before him men had confessed the particularity and sovereignty of the grace of God (having its source and standard in divine predestination) in the salvation of the elect sinner with regard to the atoning death of Christ, conversion, justification, and the preservation of the saints. These aspects of the truth of sovereign grace were taught by Augustine, Luther, Calvin, and the Synod of Dordt. Hoeksema applied the truth of

God's particular, sovereign grace to the preaching of the gospel—the actual power that realizes the purpose of election, bestows the benefits of the cross, and accomplishes conversion, justification, and preservation. Not only was the cross particular, sovereign grace ("limited atonement"), not only is the grace of regeneration, justification, and preservation particular and sovereign, not only is Jesus Christ himself in his office as mediator of the covenant and in all his work as Savior particular—a Jesus Christ for the elect only, not for all men—but also the preaching of the gospel of this Jesus Christ, of this cross, and of this salvation is particular, sovereign grace.

As Berkouwer noted, Hoeksema viewed the preaching of the gospel in the light of God's predestination. God has the gospel of Jesus Christ preached promiscuously and without discrimination to reprobate and elect. By the gospel, he shows all—in their heads and even sometimes in their emotions—reprobate and elect, their great need of salvation and the only way of salvation, namely, believing on Jesus. In the preaching, God commands, or externally calls, all to repent and believe, promising that everyone who does believe will be saved. But his gracious purpose, his loving will, his saving intention, his sincere desire, his effectual "wish" is to save the elect in the audience, and them only. The Spirit of Jesus Christ makes the preaching a mighty power of grace in the hearts of the elect, and them only.

Predestination governs the preaching of the gospel. The preaching of the gospel is grace to the elect, and to the elect only. "As many as were ordained to eternal life believed" (Acts 13:48).

In keeping with the rigorous historical fact that development of the truth always occurs by means of controversy, Hoeksema developed the truth of the preaching as sovereign, particular grace against the teaching that the preaching is a "well-meant offer of grace" to all who hear. This is the teaching that, although God's grace is particular in predestination, in the death of Christ, and even in regeneration, in the preaching of the gospel it suddenly, strangely, and utterly contradictorily becomes universal. The preaching of the gospel is grace for everybody, reprobate as well as elect. In the preaching of the gospel God wants to save everybody, reprobate as well as elect. In the preaching of the gospel, God loves everybody, reprobate as well as elect. In the preaching of the gospel, God actually tries to save everybody, reprobate as well as elect. Inasmuch as God's grace in the preaching is universal, it is also necessarily resistible. Grace no longer is sovereign.

This doctrine of preaching—the "well-meant offer"—prevailed in the Christian Reformed Church. The first (and main!) point of that church's official decisions of 1924 adopting the theory of common grace as binding church dogma confessed—and confesses—the "well-meant offer." Today, the doctrine and practice of the "well-meant offer," which flatly contradicts, weakens, and eventually corrupts everything these churches profess concerning salvation by grace alone, prevail in virtually all the Reformed, Presbyterian, and "Calvinistic" churches in North America and Great Britain.

Chapter 2

DEVELOPMENT
OF THE COVENANT

Hoeksema also developed the doctrine of the covenant. This is the doctrine that is central to the message of scripture and dear to the Reformed churches. In one important respect, this too was consistent development of the truth of salvation by grace alone, in accordance with the decree of election. Hoeksema simply applied the Canons of Dordt to the truth of the covenant.

Hoeksema taught that God establishes his covenant with Christ as the head of the covenant of grace and with the elect church, whose members are all true believers and their elect children, as his body. "Now to Abraham and his seed were the promises [of the covenant] made. He saith not, And to seeds, as of many; but as of one, And to thy seed, which is Christ...And if ye be Christ's, then are ye Abraham's seed, and heirs according to the promise" (Gal. 3:16, 29).

Regarding the covenant with the children of godly parents, the basis and meaning of infant baptism, Hoeksema taught that the covenant promise, the covenant itself, and covenant salvation are for the elect children only. In the clear language of Romans 9:8, only "the children of the promise are counted for the seed," not the "children of the flesh." The covenant, therefore, is unconditional. It depends for its establishment, maintenance, and perfection only upon the sovereign grace of God, whose source is unconditional election. The covenant is not grace for all the physical children alike, which grace would then both depend for its saving effect upon the faith and obedience of the children and be resistible and losable.

In another, equally important respect, Hoeksema's development of the truth of the covenant consisted of viewing the covenant as essentially a living bond of fellowship between Christ and the church and between Christ and each elect believer personally. Hoeksema located the ultimate source of the covenant in the very life of the triune God himself. He explained the life of God as the eternal communion of the Father and the Son in the Holy Spirit. The covenant of grace, by the decree of the triune God, is God's taking of the elect church into his own family-life in Jesus Christ by the Holy Spirit. The covenant then is not merely a means to get the elect saved, but salvation itself, the greatest good for men and women, and supreme bliss.

This development of covenant doctrine was monumental and marvelous. The truth and experience of the covenant as fellowship with the ever-blessed God are the peculiar riches of the Protestant Reformed Churches and their members.

And, we are delighted to observe, of late the riches of other Reformed churches as well.

Here is a curious thing. In the past, indeed the not-too-distant past, the prevailing, if not only, conception of the covenant in Reformed and Presbyterian churches was that the covenant is a cold and sterile contract, a business-like agreement, a threatening promise and demand, that is, a promise of God dependent on compliance with the demand by men.

In recent times, a radical change in the conception of the covenant has been taking place. On every hand, the covenant is now being described as a bond, as fellowship, as a living relationship of love. Indeed, some Reformed theologians have lately begun to trace the covenant to the triune life of God. The language of contract has virtually disappeared from the vocabulary of the covenant.

We Protestant Reformed people rejoice at this change in the prevailing covenant conception.

But we notice that there is hardly a word of acknowledgment that the Reformed theologian Herman Hoeksema was teaching this conception of the covenant eighty years ago, when he had the weight of the entire Reformed church-world against him. Much less is there any acknowledgment of Hoeksema's influence in the forming of the new conception of the covenant. Theologians who are ready to footnote a cough they make while writing will not reference Hoeksema's *Reformed Dogmatics* or *Believers and Their Seed*. Indeed, there are writings on the covenant and the Trinity that border on plagiarism of Hoeksema and of other Protestant Reformed writers who are developing and applying the doctrine of the covenant as fellowship with God that acknowledge no debt to those whose work they are using.

Regardless of this lack of grace on the part of the theologians, these "new insights" into the covenant indicate the greatness of Herman Hoeksema as a theologian.

Defense of the Faith

In addition, Hoeksema was a great man in that he defended the truth—not just the truth as he saw it, but the truth—against its adversaries, and suffered greatly for his defense.

He was a man of courage.

Courageously, he defended the truth of sovereign, particular grace against the intrusion of the lie of universal, resistible grace—"common grace" to all humans without exception and saving grace to all who come under the preaching of the gospel. His defense of the gospel cost him his already prominent position in the Christian Reformed Church in 1924 and his name in the Reformed community to this day.

In his commentary on Revelation, Hoeksema remarked, wistfully, that it would be a privilege to be among those who may confess Christ even unto death in the time of Antichrist. With the humility characteristic of the man, he quickly observed that only special saints may enjoy this privilege. He was regretting that he could not be a martyr.

But in a rare lapse of perception he was mistaken. There are other ways to lose one's life for Christ's sake than by shedding blood. Hoeksema's enemies killed him ecclesiastically. They cast him out. They killed him by defaming his good name, worldwide—hyper-Calvinist!—which is more painful than physical death.

Yet these very enemies could not help admiring Hoeksema for his courage. Back in the late 1970s, when the "conservatives" were still numerous in the Christian Reformed Church, an older Christian Reformed minister, then at the center of the life of the Christian Reformed Church, told me that it was the settled policy of the Christian Reformed ministers from 1924 on to ignore Hoeksema publicly. "However," he added, "we ministers are not together for fifteen minutes before we are talking about him." "Why?" I asked. "Why do you find yourselves bringing up Hoeksema fifty years and more after you put him out?" His answer was that Hoeksema fascinated them as a man who was willing to give up everything for the sake of what he confessed.

Courageously, Hoeksema defended the gospel of salvation by discriminating, almighty grace in the fierce, internal struggle of the Protestant Reformed Churches over the covenant in the late 1940s and early 1950s. The issue was simply the relation of the covenant and its salvation to divine election. Though it cost him two thirds of his own congregation and more than half of the members of the denomination, Hoeksema contended for the covenant of sovereign grace. He could not have done otherwise, for it was his heart's conviction that the doctrine of a covenant established by grace with all the children alike, dependent for its continuance and final salvation upon conditions performed by the children, is, as he often said, nothing but "Arminianism in the covenant."

God has proved him right in recent history.

Prophetic

This is another aspect of the man's greatness, that he was prophetic.

He warned the Christian Reformed Church in North America and the Reformed Churches in the Netherlands (GKN) during the common grace struggle in the 1920s and 1930s that the doctrine of common grace would bring the ungodly world into those churches on the floodtide. A work of grace in the ungodly whose purpose is to warrant and mandate the church's cooperation with the world in building an earthly kingdom of God and the believer's union with unbelievers in order to create a good and godly culture must corrupt the church and believer. It will break down the biblical antithesis, which is rooted in God's eternal, double predestination effecting the fundamental division of the human race into two, separate, hostile, warring kingdoms.

It has.

The doctrine of common grace with the mentality that created it, loved it, defended it, and practiced it has destroyed the Free University of Amsterdam spiritually. That once grand institution, founded on "Reformed principles," has abandoned the last vestige of the Reformed faith. It is now a spiritual wasteland and Babylon, where are "wild beasts of the desert...[It is] full of doleful creatures...and satyrs...dance there" (Isa. 13:21). For among the "Reformed principles" that formed the foundation was the world-conforming, world-welcoming common grace theory of Abraham Kuyper and Herman Bavinck. The "principle" of the certain destruction of that Reformed university was laid with its foundation.

The mentality and doctrine of common grace have destroyed the churches of the fathers of the doctrine—the GKN—physically, as well as spiritually. They are no more. Openness to the ungodly world and the fatal weakening of the antithesis, along with the rejection of predestination (in which Berkouwer played the leading role especially with his book, *Divine Election* [1956]), brought the GKN, inevitably, into the Protestant Church in the Netherlands (PKN). This is a denomination without the Reformed creedal basis, welcoming of syncretism and open unbelief, and constitutionally committed to approving homosexual acts and relations.

The GKN chose for the ungodly world. God has given those churches the world they wanted, as once in his wrath he gave Israel the quails they sinfully desired—so that they choke on the object of their lust.

More urgently and often did Hoeksema warn the Christian Reformed Church of the dire consequences of their dear theory of common grace. Listen to him during the controversy of the early 1920s.

> This doctrine [of common grace], if it is not opposed, will weaken nearly all real Christian action and send a tidal wave of world-conformity through our churches...This theory [of common grace] increasingly controls life in our circles. The result of it is world-conformity. The idea of being a stranger and pilgrim on the earth gives way to world-citizenship. They [the proponents of common grace in the Christian Reformed Church] envision that by common grace everyone can live a good life in this world before the face of God, and they say it is our obligation to raise that general human world-life as high as possible. In our opinion this view can only lead to the theory of world-conformity, which is already widely evident in our daily practice.[1]

Although they rejected the warning of their prophet (as departing churches invariably do), nevertheless, the warning made the Christian Reformed Church nervous. In 1928, the synod of the Christian Reformed Church sent a grave warning against worldliness to all the congregations. It was too little, too late. Only rescission of the common grace decision of 1924 and repentance for the common grace mentality that produced the decision would have saved them. They had sowed the wind; they must reap the whirlwind. Steadily over the years, the Christian Reformed Church succumbed, with great celebrations of their progressiveness and

---

1   Henry Danhof and Herman Hoeksema, *Sin and Grace*, ed. Herman Hanko, trans. Cornelius Hanko (Grandville, MI: Reformed Free Publishing Association, 2003), 64, 69.

modernity marking every stage of the apostasy, to the world's thinking and the world's ways. The world's thinking about origins; the world's thinking about the inspiration and historical reliability of the opening chapters of Genesis; the world's ways regarding marriage, divorce, and remarriage; the world's thinking about the authoritative headship of the husband in marriage; the world's thinking about the "full equality" of women with specific application to church office; the world's ways regarding amusement, for example, movies and dancing; the world's ways on the sabbath day; the world's thinking concerning toleration of all churches (witness the recent repudiation of the Heidelberg Catechism's condemnation of the Roman Catholic Church in question and answer 80)—all these and more have ruined the once glorious Christian Reformed Church as a Reformed church of Christ.

Accompanying the ever more enthusiastic embrace of common grace was the corresponding rejection of particular grace. The denial of sovereign, particular grace implicit in the "well-meant offer" of the first point of common grace of 1924 worked itself out in the explicit denial of limited atonement by Prof. Harold Dekker in the 1960s and in the explicit denial of the double predestination of the first head of the Canons of Dordt by Dr. Harry Boer in the 1980s. Synods of the Christian Reformed Church treated these issues. They approved the gross heresies regarding salvation by grace alone. They approved them by not condemning them and disciplining the heretics. They approved them by carefully couching their minutes so that the errors and errorists would be tolerated. Significantly, both Dekker and Boer appealed to the doctrine of common grace in support of their false doctrines.

At the present time, the Christian Reformed Church openly acknowledges that it is no longer Reformed by freeing its office-bearers from (full) subscription to the Reformed confessions.

Thus a once Reformed church abandons its Reformed foundation. Thus it advertises that it is not, and does not care to be, indeed, refuses to be, Reformed.

As Herman Hoeksema had foretold.

So unbearable did the symptoms of the doctrine and mentality of common grace become in the Christian Reformed Church that finally, in the 1990s, a number left that church to form the United Reformed Churches. But they merely reacted to the symptoms, especially the feminism of women in church office; they did not repudiate the cause. They remain fully committed to the Christian Reformed doctrine of common grace with its distinctive worldview. It is understandable then that they did not join the Protestant Reformed Churches, which certainly presented themselves as true churches of Jesus Christ, faithful to the Reformed confessions and free of all the evils that offended these people in the Christian Reformed Church, but formed yet another denomination of Reformed churches in North America.

How committed the members of the United Reformed Churches are to common grace was brought home to me soon after the formation of that denomination. An old layman, prominent in those churches, informed me that he and others in Western Michigan were concerned about the high school education of their young people. "We looked into Covenant Christian High School [the high school of the Protestant Reformed people]," he said, "but we want the common grace worldview. So we will build our own high school."

Evidently, they have learned nothing from their bitter experience in the Christian Reformed Church and schools. History will prove the truth of Hoeksema's prophecy, and the reality of his warning, concerning common grace in their case also.

Chapter 3

ARMINIANISM
IN THE COVENANT

Even more dramatically than Hoeksema's prophecy of the consequences of common grace, if this is possible, has his warning about the doctrine of a conditional covenant been realized. In the late 1940s and early 1950s, the Protestant Reformed Churches endured a grievous schism. The doctrinal issue was the nature of the covenant of grace with believers and their children. Ministers introduced into the Protestant Reformed Churches the covenant doctrine of the Reformed Churches in the Netherlands ("liberated").

This doctrine teaches that God graciously promises his covenant and its salvation to all the physical children of believers alike and that he actually establishes the covenant of grace with all the children alike at their baptism, so that all the children alike are in the covenant and begin to enjoy its benefits. However, the covenant promise and the covenant itself are conditional. Whether the promise is fulfilled in the everlasting salvation of a child and whether a child remains in the covenant depend upon conditions the child himself must perform. The covenant is conditional, that is, dependent upon works of the child, namely, faith and

The Revs. Hoeksema and Ophoff in their
last days in the seminary.

faithfulness. The covenant is conditional, because the covenant and covenant salvation are not governed by God's eternal, unconditional election.

With other Protestant Reformed ministers, notably Professor G. M. Ophoff, Hoeksema opposed this doctrine of a conditional covenant. Over the course of several years, from the pulpit and lectern, in the church papers, and then in the church assemblies, Hoeksema contended that this doctrine of a conditional covenant is "Arminianism in the covenant." Just as Arminianism teaches that the preaching of the gospel, which Arminianism conceives as a "well-meant offer," is grace to all hearers, so the doctrine of a conditional covenant teaches that the promise is grace to all the children.

Just as Arminianism teaches that the salvation of the sinner depends upon a condition he must fulfill, namely, faith, so the doctrine of a conditional covenant teaches that the salvation of baptized children depends upon conditions he must fulfill, namely, faith and a life of faithfulness.

Just as Arminianism teaches that one can fall away from Christ and lose his salvation, so the doctrine of a conditional covenant teaches that children who are in the covenant and united to Christ can fall out of the covenant and fall away from Christ.

Just as Arminianism teaches that God's grace in Jesus Christ is wider, *much* wider, than only those who finally are saved, so the doctrine of a conditional covenant teaches that God's covenant grace in Jesus Christ is wider, *much* wider, than only those children in the sphere of the covenant who are finally saved.

Just as Arminianism denies that God's saving grace is governed by an eternal decree of unconditional, double predestination, so that grace is for the elect only, so the doctrine of a conditional covenant denies that God's saving, covenant grace in Jesus Christ is governed by God's eternal predestination, so that this grace is for the elect children only.

Just as Arminianism violently denies that God's eternal decree of reprobation determines that some sinners are excluded from grace and are hardened by the preaching of the gospel, so the doctrine of a conditional covenant violently denies that reprobation determines that some children of believing parents are excluded from covenant grace and are hardened by their baptism and by the word.

Just as Arminianism teaches that a universal grace of God depends for its saving efficacy and result upon a condition performed by the sinner, so the doctrine of a conditional covenant teaches that the covenant grace of God is universal in the sphere of the covenant (towards, for, and in every baptized child), but depends for its saving efficacy and outcome upon conditions that the child must perform.

Just as Arminianism teaches that God's grace in Christ is resistible, so the doctrine of a conditional covenant teaches that the covenant grace of God in Christ is resistible.

The Protestant Reformed ministers who were enamored of the doctrine of the conditional covenant vehemently denied Hoeksema's charge of Arminianism. They insisted, as did the Reformed Churches in the Netherlands ("liberated"), whose covenant doctrine they were promoting, that this doctrine of a conditional covenant only emphasizes the "responsibility of man," and is in harmony with the confessions (although the "Three Forms of Unity" nowhere teach conditional salvation and explicitly condemn as heresy the notion that salvation is conditional and the teaching that faith is a "condition"). These ministers convinced two thirds of the membership of the Protestant Reformed Churches that Hoeksema's warning was wrong.

Many of the Reformed and Presbyterian denominations in North America took note of the controversy in the Protestant Reformed Churches. They rejected Hoeksema's warning that the doctrine of a conditional covenant as taught by K. Schilder, B. Holwerda, C. Veenhof, and the Reformed Churches in the Netherlands ("liberated") is "Arminianism in the covenant." Their rejection of the Protestant Reformed theologian's warning is not surprising. These churches themselves were open to, if they did not embrace, the doctrine of a conditional covenant.

To their mortal peril!

The Coming of the Federal [Covenant] Vision

At the present time, stunning events are taking place in many of the reputedly conservative Reformed and Presbyterian churches. In these churches, including the Orthodox Presbyterian Church, the Presbyterian Church in America, and the United Reformed Churches, has appeared a doctrine of the covenant that calls itself the "federal vision." "Federal" means "covenant." This doctrine is, and claims to be, the development of the doctrine of a conditional covenant taught by Schilder and the Reformed Churches in the Netherlands ("liberated").

Openly, the federal [covenant] vision denies justification by faith alone. Openly, it denies every one of the doctrines of grace confessed by the Canons of Dordt. Openly, it denies these great truths of the gospel in the sphere of the covenant with particular reference to the baptized children of believers. The federal [covenant] vision is an open, all-out attack on justification by faith alone—the heart of the gospel—and on the inseparably related "five points of Calvinism" with regard to the covenant.

The federal [covenant] vision is open, blatant Arminianism regarding the doctrine of the covenant.

It is not my purpose here to demonstrate the heresy of the federal [covenant] vision, to give the history of the movement, or to document the actions and refusals to act of the denominational assemblies with regard to the heresy. I have done this in a recent book, *The Covenant of God and the Children of Believers: Sovereign Grace in the Covenant* (Reformed Free Publishing Association, 2005), to which I refer the interested reader.

Suffice it to say concerning the actions, or refusals to act, of the churches mentioned above that all of them have been forced to deal with the doctrines of the federal [covenant] vision at their ecclesiastical assemblies. Although some have condemned certain aspects of the federal [covenant] vision, particularly the teaching of justification by faith and works, none has taken hold of the heresy at its root, namely, the doctrine of a conditional covenant. None of the churches is willing to take hold of it at its root. None can.

The federal [covenant] vision is genuine, logical, necessary, inevitable development of the doctrine of a conditional covenant as taught by Schilder, Holwerda, Veenhof, and the Reformed Churches in the Netherlands ("liberated"). If universal covenant grace is conditioned by the faith and faithfulness of the child, justification in the covenant is by works, and the doctrines of grace as confessed by the Canons do not apply to the covenant. If the doctrines of grace do not apply to the covenant, the errors condemned by Dordt do apply to the covenant. And the reputedly conservative Reformed and Presbyterian churches in North America approve, if they are not committed to, the doctrine of a conditional covenant.

At the same time as these astounding events are unfolding in the Reformed and Presbyterian churches in North America—*churches bound by solemn vow to the Canons of Dordt or the Westminster Confession of Faith*—theologians of the Reformed Churches in the Netherlands ("liberated") are openly criticizing the doctrine of predestination as confessed by the Canons of Dordt. They are criticizing predestination because it does not harmonize with the doctrine of a conditional covenant as held by the Reformed Churches in the Netherlands ("liberated"). Spokesmen of these churches are now publicly admitting that leading theologians of the Reformed Churches in the Netherlands ("liberated") have been criticizing the doctrine of predestination as confessed by the Canons from the very beginning of the "liberation" in the 1940s, and that Klaas Schilder was well aware of the criticism.

As Herman Hoeksema warned.

The doctrine of a conditional covenant is "Arminianism in the covenant."

And Arminianism detests the doctrine of eternal, unconditional election as the source and standard of all salvation (whether in the covenant or on the mission field) by particular, sovereign grace.

Hoeksema was no prophet, of course, by special revelation. But he was a prophet as scripture enables every sound minister to be one. Seeing clearly into the grand truths of the Bible, and believing these truths with all his heart, he could foresee the certain consequences—the judgments of God—for churches that forsake these truths.

And, then, he was not afraid, whether on account of calculating self-interest, or on account of mistaken "ecumenicity," or on account of sheer cowardice, boldly to warn others of the evil of their doctrinal way.

Is it not always the test of the true prophet that his prophecies come true?

A Small Stage

The smallness of the place God gave him might seem to gainsay Hoeksema's greatness. His place in the church was small, very small. Expelled from the Christian Reformed Church, at that time a powerful, influential denomination among the Reformed and Presbyterian churches worldwide, Hoeksema was ostracized his lifelong by the entire Reformed community of churches. His place became still smaller after the schism in the Protestant Reformed Churches in 1953. Only a few thousand members of his own denomination remained.

How small his place was, I myself experienced. For the first two years of my seminary training, I was his only student. There we sat, in one narrow, cramped, and unattractive basement room of First Protestant Reformed Church of Grand Rapids, Michigan— the two of us. Other theologians of lesser abilities, to say nothing of their orthodoxy, were teaching scores of students in fine facilities.

The smallness of his place was not the measure of the man.

Hoeksema wrote somewhere that the church has men who are every bit as great as the greatest men of the world. The difference is only that the great men of the world have a bigger stage on which to play their role. (The church's great men will have a big stage in the world to come.)

In the life and ministry of Herman Hoeksema, it pleased God to give one of his great men a small stage. With his place, Hoeksema was content.

Of this man, I have some remembrances.

Members of the Protestant Reformed Churches, who honor this man for the truth's sake, will appreciate these recollections. Members of other churches who may have no knowledge of the Protestant Reformed Churches but who love the church of Christ will find these remembrances instructive and even moving.

In the events will appear something of the true greatness of the man.

Chapter 4

———

MEMORIES
OF CHILDHOOD

My earliest memory of the man, Herman Hoeksema, hardly counts. It goes back to the middle 1940s when I was six or seven years old. A member of Hope Protestant Reformed Church, I would spend a couple of weeks in the summer with Grandpa Jasper Koole, his two daughters, Winifred and Thelma, and his two sons, Peter and John. They were members of First Protestant Reformed Church in Grand Rapids.

We walked some two miles to church from the narrow alley, Batavia Place, off Fulton Street on the northeast side of the city (Grandpa Koole was far too poor ever to have a car). As we neared the church building, coming from the north on Fuller Avenue, an astounding scene unfolded before the child, accustomed as he was to gathering for worship in the sparsely populated farm country of the Riverbend area. Fuller Avenue and the streets in all directions were filled with people, thousands of people, old men and old women, families, young people, boys and girls. All were obviously dressed for worship. All were walking to church. All seemed to the boy to be pouring into the massive building at the corner of Fuller and Franklin that was the place of worship of First Protestant Reformed Church.

First Protestant Reformed
Church

First Protestant Reformed
Church parsonage

First PR Church inside

Astonishment became amazement inside the great brick building. The vast space and beautiful interior were impressive to one used to worshipping in the small, plain, white, frame building on Wilson Avenue.

But the size of the congregation! Looking down from the heights of the back balcony, where Grandpa Koole tucked his family out of the way and out of sight as much as possible, I marveled at the size of the congregation, a veritable throng of worshippers. Five hundred families and nearly two thousand members made up the congregation in those halcyon days. Hope had fewer than twenty-five families.

Suddenly, a door in the front of the auditorium opened, and a seemingly endless stream of men flowed out—the consistory. When a man—a small figure from high up in the back balcony—took his place behind the pulpit, Grandpa leaned over to inform me in a whisper laced with utmost respect, "That's Rev. Hoeksema."

This must be the greatest church in the world, I thought.

And Rev. Hoeksema must be the greatest minister.

Hoeksema for President

A few years later, as an eighth grader at Hope Protestant Reformed Christian School, in 1952, I put Hoeksema's name in nomination for president of the United States. Well, not exactly. It was Alice Reitsma's doing—the outstanding teacher of the upper grades at Hope and ardent admirer of her pastor, the Rev. Herman Hoeksema. She proposed, in that election year, that I give a speech to the regular meeting of the Hope PTA. The main thesis of my speech would be the necessity of a Reformed, Christian man's running for the presidency. The only slightly secondary thesis would be that that man should be Herman Hoeksema. When Miss Reitsma proposed, we students disposed, partly out of love and partly out of a godly but very real fear. I gave the speech, largely drafted by my speechwriter and full of praise for the abilities of her minister.

For one night, there was a boomlet of at least two for "Hoeksema for president"—Alice Reitsma and me. The responsibility for not forming a Reformed political party and running Herman Hoeksema for president will forever reside with the Hope parents. Dwight David Eisenhower won the presidency.

Years later, sitting in class at seminary as Hoeksema criticized Abraham Kuyper for abandoning the ministry to run for political office in the Netherlands, I briefly entertained the temptation to inform him that he himself was once put up for the highest political office in the land. I thought better of it.

Hoeksema at Hope

Not long after the abortive effort to thrust Hoeksema into the political realm, I had my first real contact with the man, and took his measure as best a thirteen-year old boy could. It was the late spring of 1953, a date indelibly stamped on the history of the Protestant Reformed Churches and burned into the soul of every one who lived through that fateful year. Rev. Herman Hoeksema came to preach the Sunday evening service at the Hope Protestant Reformed Church, in the country southwest of Grand Rapids.

This was a rare and notable occurrence. It was rare because Hoeksema never preached at Hope, at least not in the memory of this thirteen-year old church member. It was notable because Hoeksema was a household name throughout the Protestant Reformed Churches, and highly regarded in the boy's family. It was as though, twenty-five years after the Reformation, Luther were to visit for the first time a little burg in the German countryside that loved the Reformer's gospel.

Even a young teenager, whose spiritual and theological interests competed with sports (and by no means always victoriously), sensed why the famous preacher was coming to Hope. The times were fraught with doctrinal and ecclesiastical controversy—of all warfare the most passionate. Rumor had wings throughout the Protestant Reformed denomination: First Church was divided; a split in the denomination was impending. Family gatherings, formerly peaceful and happy, broke up in angry shouts and crying women, to the consternation and fear of the children. Friends and families in the closely knit congregation of Hope that had worked together, for example, in establishing the school a few years earlier, visited regularly, and vacationed together no longer had anything to do with each other, apart from the requisite worship on the Lord's Day.

The worship services were tense. Not many Sundays before Hoeksema came to preach, a fierce and noisy conflict had broken out on the Hope churchyard immediately after the morning service. Prof. G. M. Ophoff had preached for the Rev. John A. Heys, Hope's pastor, as a guest minister. His sermon, like every other sermon preached at Hope in those days, condemned "conditions," "a conditional promise," "a conditional covenant," and "conditional salvation." Hardly had Ophoff exited the building than a prominent member of Hope challenged the professor's sermon, at least, its application to the conditional theology of those promoting conditions in the Protestant Reformed Churches. At once, Elder Richard Newhouse, who was accompanying Ophoff like a one-man bodyguard, sprang to Ophoff's defense.

A founding father of the Hope congregation at the time of the common grace controversy in the Christian Reformed Church in 1924, Newhouse was the embodiment of the Dutch description of a certain military hero (perhaps, Piet Hein), "*klein maar dapper*" (small but brave). Newhouse could not have reached five feet five or six inches in height in his wooden shoes. But he was an intrepid and indomitable defender of a great and sovereign God, and of Prof. G. M. Ophoff. Hoeksema, Newhouse respected; Ophoff, the first pastor of Hope and the man with whom Newhouse went through the common grace wars, he loved.

Stories about the "little Dutchman" of Hope are legion in the bend of the Grand River to the west and Lake Michigan. They are all true, and they are all good. Newhouse was one of Hope's great men, exemplifying the way of God with his church in calling the foolish, weak, and base, in order to confound the things that are mighty (1 Cor. 1:25–31). We remember him with honor and affection.

Shortly before the founding of Hope Protestant Reformed Church, when the controversy over common grace was raging in the Christian Reformed Church, Prof. Samuel Volbeda preached for the Hope Christian Reformed Church in Riverbend, where Newhouse was member. Volbeda's sermon was a ringing defense of salvation by sovereign, particular grace. This was the kind of sermon that stirred Newhouse to the depths of his soul. "*God moet alles zijn; de mens niets*" ("God must be everything; man, nothing"). Nevertheless, after the service, the doughty Dutchman, whose occupation was that of a lowly "string-butcher" and whose education never went beyond the third grade, accosted the learned, aristocratic professor: "Why do you always come to Hope with a sermon on the sovereignty of God, when you will not defend Hoeksema and Danhof, who stand for God's sovereignty, in the papers and assemblies of the churches?"

For a few years after its organization as a congregation in 1916, the Hope Christian Reformed Church (out of which the Hope Protestant Reformed Church would be born in 1924) held its worship services in Newhouse's home. During the hot summer months, the congregation would hold the afternoon service outdoors, in Newhouse's yard, beneath the spreading branches of a large tree.

On one occasion, in the midst of the afternoon service, a thunderstorm developed quickly in the southwestern sky. As the billowing clouds approached the worshipping congregation, a loud clap of thunder rumbled across Kenowa Avenue over the worshippers. The preacher that afternoon was a nervous seminarian. He paused, mid-way through his sermon, and asked, "What shall I do?" Came back at once the reply from Newhouse, "Keep on preaching!"

Once, and once only, in later years, did the perennial elder teach catechism. By every standard of proper catechetics, the class was a disaster. The opening prayer was half-English, half-Dutch. After asking the questions of the lesson on Reformed doctrine from the book, Newhouse began an explanation of the lesson in English. Within five minutes, he had lapsed into the Dutch language, his native tongue and the language in which he thought. After a few minutes of Dutch, the realization hit him that the class could not understand a word he was saying. Abruptly, he said (in English), "Let us pray," and prayed a closing prayer (in Dutch).

Class dismissed.

A failure, by men's standards.

But not, in reality.

For God, who delights in making straight lines with crooked sticks, blessed that strange, fifteen-minute class in Reformed doctrine to a class of sixteen-year old catechism students, who knew very well that the class was a botch. The opening Psalter number was Newhouse's favorite, Psalter number 367 (all the stanzas), "Gracious Lord, remember David." He sang it with obvious devotion to his great God, oblivious to the twelve or fifteen catechumens. His prayer was fervent—sheer worship of the God who was there—both the English and the Dutch components. And even the Dutch had its familiar word, "*Heere*."

The five or ten minute "exposition," which may or may not

have been on the precise topic of the lesson, was praise of the mighty and gracious father of Jesus Christ.

There was no mockery by the students. There was no laughter during the class, or after. Not one of the students said one demeaning word as we trooped up the steps from the basement of the church building. No doubt, one reason was that we respected and loved the old man as our elder. The chief reason, I now realize, was that we had been, in an odd way, in the presence of God, and we felt it.

But he never taught again, and this was right. Standards of catechetics are necessary. And God usually makes straight lines with straight sticks.

Now, on this Sabbath morning, the little fighter took up the cudgels for Prof. Ophoff and for the sovereignty of covenant grace against his own fellow church member, who, truth to tell, may only have been seeking clarification. Ophoff never said a word. The battle was pitched. With all the rest of the congregation, we teenagers and children watched and listened with mounting trepidation and growing awareness that our church-world—vital to us already at that age—was being shaken.

A short time later, Richard Newhouse would be one of the two elders who gave a report to Classis East of the Protestant Reformed Churches condemning the doctrine of a conditional covenant, to the saving of the Protestant Reformed Churches.

In that highly charged atmosphere, the Rev. Herman Hoeksema climbed the platform in the small, frame church building on Wilson

Picture from December 1959 *Beacon Lights* for outlines on the Book of Revelation.

Avenue. that Sunday evening in early 1953. Two physical features of the man registered with me: his powerful build and his iron-gray hair. One spiritual characteristic struck me: his authority.

In those days, the order of worship was the reading of scripture before the congregational prayer. The chapter was Ephesians 4. Verse 14 of the chapter reads: "That we henceforth be no more children, tossed to and fro, and carried about with every wind of doctrine, by the sleight of men, and cunning craftiness, whereby they lie in wait to deceive." Although there was no announcement of the text in the bulletin (Hoeksema was a visiting preacher) and although Hoeksema did not reveal his text before reading the chapter, I knew without any doubt, as did everyone else in the audience, the text he intended to preach—verse 14, a warning against being carried about with every wind of doctrine, that is, the doctrine of a conditional covenant.

After the congregational prayer, the collection, and the singing of another psalm, the remarkable, memorable thing happened. Hoeksema came to the pulpit, looked us over, and said this: "I had intended when I came here tonight to preach on verse 14 of Ephesians 4, because of the present serious troubles in our churches. But I have changed my mind. There are so many children and young people in the Hope congregation that I have decided that my sermon on Ephesians 4:14 would not be fitting. Therefore, I am going to preach a different sermon."

Whereupon he read a brief passage from John 10 and preached a sermon on Jesus as the good shepherd. There was not a word in the sermon about conditions, or a conditional covenant.

Hoeksema's behavior that night long ago left two powerful impressions. The first was that this must be an extraordinary preacher, who could come up with another sermon than he intended to give, on the spot. The second was that the evil reports being spread by his enemies in the churches were false. He was not the hard and unloving man they made him out to be in their campaign of whispering behind his back. In the midst of struggle over everything he believed, worked for, suffered for, and built, he showed a shepherd's concern for the children and young people of the Hope congregation.

Chapter 5

———

A PASTORAL HEART

Although a profound theologian, learned scholar, and formidable controversialist, Herman Hoeksema had the heart of a pastor. His published sermons demonstrate the love of a shepherd for the people of God, especially his own congregation, First Protestant Reformed Church of Grand Rapids, Michigan.

This came home to me many years after Hoeksema's death when I was editing his series of sermons on Romans for publication as *Righteous by Faith Alone: A Devotional Commentary on Romans*. The series of sermons, as he preached it in First Church in the late 1930s, had two grand themes. They ran through the sermons from beginning to end. One was the glory of God as revealed in the gospel of justification by faith alone.

The other, hardly less prominent, was the comfort of every believer by this gospel of justification. Again and again, Hoeksema explicitly applied the gospel-truth of righteousness by faith alone to the burdened souls of the members of the congregation, struggling with the guilt of their sins and fearful of the wrath of God to which their transgressions and corruption exposed them.

Against the "Further Reformation"

Especially did Herman Hoeksema the pastoral preacher exert himself to deliver members of his congregation from the doubt that was then, and still is today, perversely promoted and even praised by disciples of the Puritans. These are the contemporary representatives and advocates of the movement in the Netherlands in the seventeenth century that called itself the *"nadere reformatie"* ("further reformation"). Falsely charging the Reformation of the sixteenth century with having failed to do justice to the experience of salvation, this

With grandchild, Anita

movement arrogantly took upon itself the responsibility of completing the unfinished Reformation.

Rather than completing, or even developing, the Reformation, however, the movement of the "further reformation" radically deviated from the Reformation. Whereas, for assurance of salvation, the Reformation directed the faith of the elect believer to Jesus Christ as presented in the preaching of the doctrine of the gospel, outside the believer, the "further reformation" turned the believer in on himself, to his own mysterious, mystical experiences, or feelings. The result was doubt, doubt on a huge scale, doubt that afflicted the vast majority of the members of the congregations (even though they confessed themselves believers), doubt that lasted for years, doubt in which many eventually died (with all the terror that must accompany dying without assurance of salvation).

The Puritans and their theological disciples in the "further reformation" denied that true, justifying faith in Jesus Christ as proclaimed in the gospel is assurance of salvation, as is the teaching of question and answer 21 of the Heidelberg Catechism. Assurance of one's own salvation comes to a believer, if it comes at all, only after the believer has struggled with doubt—prevailing, terrifying, hellish doubt—for many years. If a believer does finally obtain assurance (and only a few of God's favorite children ever do!), he gets it, not by believing only in Jesus Christ, but through an extraordinary, mystical experience, which he himself has labored to bring about.

In Hoeksema's day, those in North America whose theology thus robbed confessing believers of the comfort of assurance were the theologians, ministers, and teachers of the Netherlands Reformed congregations. Today, this is also true of the Heritage Reformed congregations.

It is obvious in the Romans sermons that Hoeksema knew that some in his congregation were afflicted with the Puritan disease of doubt and the related disease of grounding assurance of salvation upon the broken reed of a mystical experience. Hoeksema called the disease "sickly mysticism." As a good undershepherd of Jesus Christ, Hoeksema could not tolerate this spiritual sickness. He certainly did not excuse it. Much less did he promote it. Rather, he probed the sore in order to heal it with the balm of the gospel of justification by faith alone.

Preaching Romans 7:24–25a, "The Wretched Christian," Hoeksema observed that the text teaches that the "wretched Christian seeks deliverance" ("who shall deliver me?"). Then he exposed the disease of doubt:

There is [a] type of people who do not seek. They are a sickly kind of people. They are people who have a certain sickly knowledge of sin. They are people who leave the impression that they rejoice in the fact that they are able to say that they are so miserable. You can recognize these people by the fact that they always stop there. They say, "O wretched man that I am!" And there they stop. They do not seek. This is not the apostle. If one knows his misery, he seeks spontaneously.[1]

Immediately, Hoeksema added: "And he finds." This too was directed against the miserable Puritan and "further reformation" doctrine, which teaches that many, if not most, believers seek the deliverance of assurance all their lives without ever finding it.

A man once said to me that he had been seeking all his life. I told him that was not true. Scripture says that he who seeks shall surely find. This man said, "Yes, but in God's time." I answered, "Yes, and God's time is, 'Before they call, I will answer them.'" This surely follows. You cannot ask the question without the answer being there. If you seek, you shall surely find.[2]

As a good pastor, Hoeksema warned against seeking deliverance from sin, including assurance of deliverance, in the wrong, Puritan and "further reformation" way.

How do you seek [deliverance]? There is only one way: in the Word of God. Some people would like to have an

---

1 Herman Hoeksema, *Righteous by Faith Alone: A Devotional Commentary on Romans*, ed. David J. Engelsma (Grandville, MI: Reformed Free Publishing Association, 2002), 299–300.

2 Hoeksema, *Righteous by Faith Alone*, 300.

angel come down from heaven to tell them. That cannot be. Others would like to have a certain word, or a certain experience. But it is a seeking outside of the Word of God. These people do not find. You cannot find God outside of the Word. But if you seek the answer to the question "Who shall deliver me?" in the Bible, you will find the answer.[3]

When he explained the outstanding passage of scripture on assurance of salvation, Romans 8:15–16, Hoeksema again pointedly warned his flock against the teaching of assurance that produces doubt. The text reads: "Ye have received the Spirit of adoption, whereby we cry, Abba, Father. The Spirit itself beareth witness with our spirit, that we are the children of God." Hoeksema posed the question, "How does the Spirit do this?" that is, give all believers and their children "assurance…that we are children of God." He answered his question, negatively, combating (as his answer indicates to every one who is in the least familiar with Puritan and "further reformation" doctrine) the proposed way of assurance of Puritanism:

> [The Spirit] does not do it [give assurance of sonship and salvation] in a fanatical way, nor does He do it in a mystical way. Some teach that the Spirit directly, mystically, audibly, tells every child of God, outside of the Word, that he is a child of God. But there is no such thing. I never heard such whisperings of the Spirit in my heart. And if I did hear such whisperings, I would not trust them. I could not be sure that these whisperings were not the testimony of some other spirit. The Spirit never says anything outside

---

3   Hoeksema, *Righteous by Faith Alone*, 301.

the Word…Not directly, but through the Word, this testimony comes to us.[4]

Showing thorough knowledge of the Puritan and "further reformation" doctrine of doubt and demonstrating a good pastor's determination that this doctrine not take root in his congregation, and be rooted up where it might have lodged, Hoeksema added something to his negative answer.

But even then we must be careful. Some people, when they say that this testimony comes to us through the Word, mean that the Spirit at a certain time comes with a certain text. This is not true. I do not mean to say that the Spirit never comes with a certain text, at a certain time, and under certain circumstances. But I mean this: your assurance cannot rest on that. The Spirit does not work through a certain text, but He works through the *whole* Word of God. It is through the whole of Scripture that the Spirit bears this testimony.[5]

Hoeksema was referring to the mystical notion and practice that one gets assurance of salvation by letting his Bible fall open at random and blindly stabbing his finger at a text that happens to speak of salvation, or by having a stray text come into his mind, unexpectedly, as he goes about the business of his everyday life.

The Gospel of Assurance

His positive answer to the question, "How does the Spirit give assurance of salvation?" was this: "The Spirit takes the content of

---

4 Hoeksema, *Righteous by Faith Alone*, 333.
5 Hoeksema, *Righteous by Faith Alone*, 333.

the Word of God. He applies it to our hearts." The role of preaching in this assuring work of the Spirit, Hoeksema indicated in his sermon on Romans 1:16–17, his sermon on Romans 10:14–15, and his sermon on Romans 10:16–18.[6] Hoeksema added, concerning the way in which the Spirit gives assurance, that "the Spirit works assurance in the fellowship of the church and in the way of sanctification."[7]

The significance of faith in receiving assurance, Hoeksema had indicated earlier in the series of sermons on Romans. In his sermon on Romans 4:3–5, Hoeksema taught his congregation that "saving faith…reveals itself as undoubting certainty." "Saving faith is that I am certain…that I am justified."[8]

Note well the verb in the second of these quotations concerning faith: True faith *is* certainty. Denial of this fundamental truth concerning saving, justifying faith was the false doctrine of Puritanism and the "further reformation" that caused the God-dishonoring and soul-tormenting doubt of multitudes, as is the case still today with the avowed disciples of the Puritans and the "further reformation."

Herman Hoeksema's sermons expressed a pastor's heart. Is not a pastor's heart expressed in preaching that gladly obeys the divine call to the prophet, "Comfort ye, comfort ye, my people"? Is not a pastor's heart expressed by teaching that joyfully brings to the congregation the basic theme of the Heidelberg Catechism, namely, comfort in life and death for every believer and covenant child of the believer that consists of conscious belonging to Jesus Christ, because "by his Holy Spirit he also assures me of eternal life"?

---

6   Hoeksema, *Righteous by Faith Alone*, 9–15, 474–81, 482–95.
7   Hoeksema, *Righteous by Faith Alone*, 344.
8   Hoeksema, *Righteous by Faith Alone*, 143–44

Does not a pastor's heart compel the minister to war against false teaching that is destructive of the comfort of the gospel, that God wills for all his children, that all God's children have a right to, and that is necessary in order to live faithfully and to die hopefully?

Does the heart of a pastor of the flock of Christ bring a message that plunges many, even the majority, of the congregation, who profess to be believers, into doubt of their salvation; that makes assurance of salvation impossible for many of them as long as they live; that shuts them up to face death themselves, and bury loved ones, in the terror of damnation; and that assures a few on the basis of a false, deceitful, and weak ground, namely, an extraordinary experience?

Hoeksema's sermons were a public expression of the man's pastoral heart.

Chapter 6

A PASTORAL HEART
(Continued)

H erman Hoeksema had the heart of a pastor.

His sermons were a public expression of his pastoral heart, as I demonstrated in the previous chapter.

I saw this heart in Hoeksema's ministry "from house to house" (Acts 20:20).

It was the late spring of 1960.

Grandpa Jasper Koole was dying. He asked me whether Rev. Hoeksema would be willing to call on him as he, Grandpa Koole, lay on what he knew to be his deathbed. And would I make the request of Rev. Hoeksema for him. The reason he asked me was that I had just enrolled to enter the Protestant Reformed Seminary in the fall of 1960.

A Doubting Parishioner

Jasper Koole was a lifelong, faithful member of First Protestant Reformed Church in Grand Rapids, Michigan. In fact, he was a charter member of First Church. He suffered the reproach of Christ with Herman Hoeksema, the consistory, and many other members of Eastern Avenue Christian Reformed Church in being cast out of the Christian Reformed Church for the confession of the sovereign, particular grace of God in Jesus Christ.

But Jasper Koole, who believed in Jesus Christ as presented in the gospel, was plagued with doubt concerning his salvation. For many years, he remained only a baptized member of First Church. At the baptism of his first three children, Jasper Koole remained seated and silent as Bessie, his wife, stood before the large congregation of First Church, answering the questions of the baptism form and holding the children as the minister sprinkled them with water in the name of the triune God. Only when the fourth child was to be baptized was he able to make public confession of his faith and thus present his child for baptism. Jasper Koole was forty.

His children relate that when First Church celebrated the Lord's supper, their father would walk them to church from Batavia Place, see his wife and them into the sanctuary, and then disappear. For the hour and a half of the service, he would walk the streets of Grand Rapids, until the service of the holy supper was finished. Then he would appear again to walk them home. He felt himself unworthy even to be present at a worship service that included the supper of the body and the blood of the Savior.

My mother tells how, as a child, she stumbled upon her father in his bedroom, wholly unaware of her presence, on his knees at the side of the bed, groaning aloud to God over his sins.

Therein was not his weakness.

Whether we groan aloud (and this is not foreign to any believer), all believers abhor themselves on account of their sinfulness and sins. "O wretched man that I am!" (Rom. 7:24) It is no small part of our sin that we do not abhor ourselves sufficiently. We ought to be on our knees groaning over our guilt and shame more than we are. Much more.

But the weakness of Jasper Koole was his failure to trust the promise of the gospel to every penitent sinner, even such a great sinner as Jasper Koole knew himself to be (and as every one of us in fact is), that God will forgive his sins for the sake of the death of Jesus Christ.

This was a grievous weakness.

There were reasons for the weakness, reasons for doubting his salvation. Not excuses or justification, for there is no excuse or justification for the sin of unbelieving doubt. But reasons.

Grandpa Koole was a Zeelander, having emigrated with his parents to the United States from that province in the Netherlands when he was three years old. Zeelanders are given to feelings in religion. They are prone to mysticism and doubt.

Jasper Koole (1887–1960).
*From the archives
of David J. Engelsma.*

His upbringing in the home (how vital, how determinative is a child's upbringing at home! parents, take heed!) was heavily influenced by the "*nadere reformatie*" ("further reformation"), Zeeland being a very fertile field for that movement of religious feelings, with its insistence that all children of church members are unregenerated until they grow up and have an extraordinary experience; its overpowering message of the darkness of sin with hardly a note of deliverance or a ray of light for the miserable sinner in the glad tidings of the abounding grace of God in the cross of Christ; its urging of doubt of one's salvation as normal for most, if not all, church members for many years; its supercilious criticism of believers in other churches who dare to be sure of their salvation as "light," that is, superficial, people (as though assurance were a vice and doubt, a virtue); and its strong suggestion, if not blunt assertion, that the only way to be certain of salvation is the experience of an extraordinary, mysterious, mystical experience.

The gloomy and mystical Puritan theology of the "further reformation" is powerful, stubbornly resistant to the preaching of the gospel of certainty and assurance. It took years of Hoeksema's preaching of grace to heal Jasper Koole's disease of doubt. Even then, the struggle with doubt continued.

And a reason was Satan, malignant minister of doubt (as the Holy Spirit is the blessed agent of certainty), who is delighted to use a corrupted Reformed theology, bad spiritual physicians of the souls of church members, and misled parents to deprive multitudes of professing people of God of the assurance of salvation.

Now Grandpa Koole lay dying.

As the dark shadows of death deepen, our sins rise up against us in their exceeding great number and in their exceeding great evil. In the deep shadows of death appear the minions of the prince of darkness for the final assault. "Can you be a child of God? You? Remember your sins! Here they are! Look at them! Did you ever really love God? Did you ever really do anything for his sake? And if you cry out, you wretch, that you believe in Jesus, are you sure? Absolutely sure? The God who stands on the other side of your last breath, which comes quickly, awaits your entrance into eternity, to damn you."

The climactic struggle of faith against doubt.

Especially for a Zeelander, brought up to doubt, doubting for forty years, struggling with doubt all his life.

A Pastoral Call

Would Rev. Hoeksema be willing to call on him? Grandpa Koole was serious with the question. He wondered whether Rev. Hoeksema would be willing. To Grandpa Koole, Rev. Hoeksema was a great man of God, probably far too busy with important duties of the church to call on the likes of Jasper Koole. Justifiably, too busy. Grandpa Koole knew himself to be an insignificant member of First Church, as by all human standards he was. He was not sure Rev. Hoeksema would even know who he was. He mentioned that Rev. Hoeksema had never visited him at his home, at least socially (which struck me as very strange, being myself a member of a small church in which the minister visited with all the families).

I called Rev. Hoeksema. Would he pay a pastoral visit to his dying parishioner, Jasper Koole? Unsure whether he did indeed know Grandpa Koole, I began identifying my grandfather. Rev. Hoeksema interrupted me, "I know Jasper Koole. I will be over right away. Will you be there to let me in?"

Within the hour, the big car pulled up to the curb on Thomas Street. I led Rev. Hoeksema to the little bedroom where a wan and wasted Jasper Koole lay on his deathbed. Then I shut the door on the two old men, Rev. Hoeksema, age seventy-four, and my grandfather, age seventy-three.

No human knows what went on in that room. Neither Grandpa Koole nor Rev. Hoeksema ever said a word to me or to anyone else what went on between them, and between the devils of hell and the Spirit of Jesus Christ.

But today I am as sure of what was said there as if I had listened at the door.

Jasper Koole cried out in misery about his sins and in fear about his salvation.

Hoeksema heard him out.

When Grandpa Koole had finished, Hoeksema responded in the house of his parishioner, whom he loved as one of Christ's own, as he had preached Sunday after Sunday in the pulpit of First Church. I can hear Hoeksema begin by affirming that Jasper Koole was as great a sinner as he confessed himself to be, indeed, worse, far worse. There is no way to assurance of salvation by denying or minimizing sin. Then he brought to Jasper Koole, penitent sinner and believer, the promise of God himself, who cannot lie, that his sins were forgiven and blotted out for the sake of the cross of Christ, in the eternal love of God for him, so that death for Jasper Koole would be entrance into eternal life and glory.

Certainly!

Absolutely certainly!

Without any doubt!

Having read the Bible and prayed, Rev. Hoeksema went his way.

Within a month or so, Grandpa Koole died in faith's assurance of salvation.

Not without the means of a genuinely pastoral heart, a heart able and willing to bring the comfort of the gospel, both publicly from the pulpit and from house to house.

Many thousands have died, and will die, as Jasper Koole died and as God wills his beloved people to die, in the assurance of salvation and in the confidence of the resurrection, by means of the gospel—the pure, sound Reformed faith—as preached by Herman Hoeksema and by those whom he instructed.

With God, this counts for greatness.

Because it is from God.

Chapter 7

———

MAGNANIMITY

During the three years of my close contact with the Rev. Prof. Herman Hoeksema in the Protestant Reformed Seminary, I found him to be unfailingly magnanimous.

This will surprise those whose judgment of the man has been formed by the slanders of his theological and ecclesiastical foes.

It may also surprise those who conclude from Hoeksema's uncompromising defense of the gospel of grace, and sharp condemnation of theologians who deviated from it, that personally Herman Hoeksema was narrow, determined to have his own way, sensitive to any slight of, or disagreement with, himself, and ready to strike out at those who criticized him.

Magnanimity is a lovely Christian perfection.

Literally, the English word, derived from the Latin, means 'largeness of soul.' It is the grace, not only of openness to disagreement with oneself (which is not the same as tolerance of disagreement with the word of God), but also of bearing insult and abuse patiently, so that one neither reacts in anger to contradiction, nor retaliates for injury, nor becomes embittered by wrong done to himself.

The magnanimous man graciously puts up with those who hurt him.

The opposite is pettiness; sensitivity to every slight; a brooking no disagreement; and vindictiveness—smallness of soul.

The Greek word in the New Testament that refers to magnanimity is usually translated by the Authorized Version as "longsuffering." Literally, the Greek word means 'long of spirit.' This is the word translated "suffereth long" in 1 Corinthians 13:4: "Charity suffereth long." Love in one who has the Spirit of Christ expresses itself by graciously and patiently putting up with the neighbor who injures him, especially the neighbor in the church.

The virtue of magnanimity is especially necessary in a minister. The minister is exposed, more than any other, to personal criticism, slight, and abuse—real injury. Weakened, like every other human, by a sinful nature, the minister is tempted to assert himself, to strike back, and to become bitter. But the result of this pettiness, this smallness of soul and shortness of spirit, would be senseless and profitless strife in the church, a weakening of his teaching ministry, and spiritual harm to himself (bitterness corrodes the Spirit's work of grace), to say nothing of interference with the building of the kingdom of Christ.

With good reason, therefore, Paul bound upon young Pastor Timothy (and the Holy Spirit binds upon every minister, old as well as young), with solemn charge ("before God and the Lord Jesus Christ"), that he "exhort with all longsuffering" (2 Tim. 4:2).

General Magnanimity

Even his doctrinal adversaries witnessed, and were the beneficiaries of, Hoeksema's magnanimity, albeit in a peculiar manner. Richard Mouw has related to this writer the story of a meeting over lunch of the editors of the *Reformed Journal* magazine at the Schnitzelbank, Hoeksema's favorite restaurant. These editors would have included James Daane, Harold Dekker (a prominent contributing writer), Harry Boer, Henry Stob, Lester DeKoster, Lewis Smedes, and the publisher of the magazine, Bill Eerdmans. By no stretch of the imagination could these men be conceived as theological allies of Herman Hoeksema in the Christian Reformed Church. When the time came to pay the bill, Eerdmans signaled for the waitress (ministers always graciously allow the businessman to pay the bill). "Oh," said the waitress, "your bill has already been paid." "Who paid our bill?" asked Eerdmans in bewilderment. "The gentleman sitting over there," responded the waitress, pointing to a smiling, magnanimous Herman Hoeksema, waving genially to the group of Christian Reformed "liberals."

Mention of the Schnitzelbank brings to mind an incident in Hoeksema's ministry that indicates one of his virtues, and by no means the least. He was not afflicted with a desire for filthy lucre. This is especially unusual in a prestigious pastor of a very large congregation, and one with a worldwide reputation, as recent events in the American church-world indicate. His salary at First Church was always modest. On one occasion, his congregation was determined to raise his salary, if only slightly. At the meeting that would decide the issue, Hoeksema declared emphatically that he neither needed nor desired a raise. When the congregation voted to raise his salary, nevertheless, Hoeksema responded, "I guess I will have to take 'Ma' (so he always referred to his wife) to the 'Schnitz' (so he always referred to his favorite restaurant) more often."

It was at the "Schnitz" that Hoeksema called a leading defender of the doctrine of common grace publicly to account on one occasion. This defender was the Christian Reformed theologian, Prof. R[inck]. B. Kuiper. The Hoeksema's and the Kuiper's were sitting on opposite ends of the sizable dining area. The popular restaurant was full. At the time, Prof. Harold Dekker's article in the *Reformed Journal* advocating universal atonement *on the basis of the Christian Reformed Church's doctrine of common grace* had just been published. Prof. Kuiper was an ardent proponent of common grace, particularly the well-meant offer, denying Hoeksema's charge that the offer is Arminianism. Spotting Kuiper across the room, Hoeksema bellowed, with a roar that was heard throughout the room and could have been heard in the parking lot, "What do you think [of common grace, and of the long-time controversy between the two antagonists over the doctrine] now, Rinck?" "Rinck" did not respond.

Hoeksema's *Peccavi*

I saw something of the large soul of Herman Hoeksema in his response, on one occasion, to the reaction of Richard Newhouse (yes, the little Dutchman of Hope figures in our story once again) to his (Hoeksema's) "*peccavi.*"

I explain.

In the February 15, 1960 issue of the *Standard Bearer*, Hoeksema introduced his editorial with the information that the editorial would consist largely of his publishing a protest by the "Orthodox Protestant Reformed Church" (the consistory of the schismatic "First Orthodox Protestant Reformed Church" of Grand Rapids, Michigan, the president of which was the Rev. Hubert De Wolf) to their synod. (The content of the protest was sad. It indicated that the consistory was unhappy with the doctrinal compromise that their synod was making in order to be received back into the Christian Reformed Church. But this is another story.)

At the end of his brief introduction to the publishing of the protest, Editor Hoeksema wrote, "Here, then, follows the protest."

What actually followed, however, on the pages of the February 15, 1960 *Standard Bearer* was not the protest at all.

Rather, there appeared a catechism of sorts, treating the reorganization of Second Protestant Reformed Church of Grand Rapids in the turbulent days of the schism in the Protestant Reformed Churches of the 1950s and various and sundry aspects of Reformed church polity.

Obviously, the kind of printing error had been made that keeps editors awake at night in fear of its happening and that embarrasses them when it occurs.

Aggravating the mistake, and compounding the confusion, were that Hoeksema appended remarks at the end of what ought to have been, and was advertised as being, a protest (but was not) that applied to the non-existent protest, but not at all to the very real catechism. His editorial concluded, "The reader will agree with me that the above [protest] is a thoroughly Protestant Reformed document."

An explanation of the glaring mistake would be necessary.

The explanation was forthcoming in the next issue of the *Standard Bearer* (March 1, 1960). It read as follows:

All our readers, no doubt, will by this time have wondered about my editorial in the Feb. 15 issue of our paper. The explanation is that, instead of the protest I meant to publish, something else appeared and the protest was left out. Hence I now publish the entire editorial as I meant to write it.

You ask who is to blame for this ridiculous error. Let us say: the undersigned, although he still cannot understand how it could possibly have taken place.

Just remember, dear reader, that *nihil humanum alienum est mihi*. And I say *peccavi*. Perhaps you cannot figure this out either. Then you better ask someone that knows Latin.[9]

Finally, the elusive protest did, in fact, appear.
"*Peccavi*"—Latin for 'I have erred.'
Hoeksema's "*peccavi.*"
There would be one "dear reader" who would not so easily be placated by Hoeksema's "*peccavi.*"

At that time, still in college, I worked for a farmer in the River-bend area, who also employed Richard Newhouse, the venerable elder of Hope Protestant Reformed Church in what is now Walker, Michigan. Newhouse, a widower, lived in a trailer on the farm, in the shade of a large apple tree. Often, of an early evening, after milking, I would walk over to the trailer, to visit with Mr. New-house, whose company and conversation I greatly enjoyed.

Richard Newhouse abroad (in Loveland, Colorado) with friends in 1966.
From the archives of David J. Engelsma.

---

9   Herman Hoeksema, "As to Being Protestant Reformed," *Standard Bearer* 36, no. 11 (March 1, 1960): 244–246.

One evening, soon after March 1, 1960, I discovered an agitated Dutchman. Newhouse sat on a raised platform (otherwise the short man could not see out of the windows of his trailer), seated in his big, overstuffed chair (very much like a little lord on his large throne), waving the latest issue of the *Standard Bearer* (next to the Bible his favorite and most authoritative reading).

There was no polite greeting, no question about the cows, no inquiry after my studies.

Rather, an abrupt, "*Wat is dit? Wat is dit?*"

"*Peccaaavi!*" "*Peccaaavi!*" "*Peccaaavi!*" (Thus he grossly mispronounced the Latin.)

With some academic pride, I fear, I could explain to him that "*peccavi*" (I took pains to correct his pronunciation by my own careful enunciation—a completely wasted effort) was Latin for "I have erred," or, "I have made a mistake."

If I expected some praise for, or even recognition of, my knowledge of a foreign language, I would quickly be disabused of the notion.

Newhouse paused for a moment to digest the information, and exclaimed, "*Peccaaavi! Peccaaavi!* It took him forty years to admit he made a mistake, and then he did it in a language nobody can understand."

Young and naïve, I filed this bon mot for specific, future use. The near future.

Hoeksema's Large Soul

In the fall of the same year, I began my seminary studies with Prof. Herman Hoeksema. Not long after the start of the school-year, during coffee break in the kitchen of the old First Church at the corner of Fuller and Franklin, as Hoeksema was lighting his massive pipe, pleasurably filling his lungs (and the room) with clouds of smoke, I asked him, casually, "Do you know Richard Newhouse?"

"Do I know Richard Newhouse?" he responded. "I know Richard Newhouse."

Whereupon I related, with gusto, the tale of Newhouse's reaction to my professor's "*peccavi*," concluding with an enthusiastic, full quotation of Newhouse's "it took him forty years to admit that he made a mistake," etc.

As I reflect today on my temerity, there comes to mind the proverb, "Fools rush in where angels fear to tread."

Of course, Hoeksema did know Newhouse—a wholehearted, lifelong supporter and friend. But even then…

And Hoeksema did not know me, except as a fledgling seminarian, and apparently cheeky.

A man with a small soul would have put me in my place, and perhaps Richard Newhouse too, with a withering look or a cutting remark, and likely both.

Hoeksema did no such thing.

He threw his head back and roared with laughter, hard and long.

"You say hello to Newhouse for me. And you tell him that he ought to learn some Latin" (which I did).

There was no defensiveness, no sensitivity to what could easily have been taken as an insult, no involuntary anger, no striking back against a perceived slight (or against the "slighters"), no putting of lesser folk in their place, not even a struggle to gain his composure.

Magnanimity!

In the remark by Newhouse, to which Hoeksema responded with magnanimity, there was more than meets the eye.

That "more" brings to light another aspect of Hoeksema's greatness.

Chapter 8

A GOD-GIVEN LEADER

In Richard Newhouse's response to Herman Hoeksema's "*pec-cavi*" ("I have erred"), "It took him forty years to admit he made a mistake, and then he did it in a language nobody can understand," there was more than met the eye.

The remark reflected the awareness of the members of the Protestant Reformed Churches that Hoeksema was never wrong.

I do not at all refer to his spiritual life. He was a sinful man, with only a small beginning of the new obedience. He confessed this in his congregational prayers, in his sermons, and in all his writings. No theologian humbled the elect sinner, including, of course, himself, more deeply than did Hoeksema. He taught the total depravity of the natural man, unmitigated by common grace; the continuing total depravity of the regenerated child of God *by nature* to the end of his days, rightly applying Romans 7:24 to the believer; the defiling of every good work of the saint with sin; and the grace of God as the source of all good in the Christian.

He mentioned to me once, offhandedly, that his private prayer on the platform at church, in preparation for preaching, always was, "I repent of all my sins; forgive me." "Offhandedly," but with the unmistakable purpose that I should do the same.

The pastor in his study, from *Therefore Have I Spoken*, p. 131.

Nor do I refer to his personal dealings with others in his everyday life. About this I know very little, and care less. But I do note that I found his dealings with me and with others courteous and brotherly during the three years of my contact with him in the seminary. By all accounts, his conduct in his marriage and family was exemplary. No one could ever blame him for a fault that disqualified him for the ministry. With the rarest exception, during all the long and bitter controversy in the late 1940s and early 1950s, that threatened the very existence of the churches he loved and that must have well-nigh killed him, he stuck doggedly to the doctrinal issue, while his opponents were relentlessly attacking his person.

Almost Always Right

But I refer to his public stands for truth and righteousness, his public instruction to the churches, and his public advice regarding important cases and issues in the churches, whether from the pulpit, in the *Standard Bearer*, in his many books and pamphlets, and at the church assemblies. Throughout his entire, long ministry, he was never, or almost never, wrong. Never did he have to say, "I have erred," whether in English, Dutch, or Latin. Never did he have to recant a position he had taken. Never did he have to admit that he had misled the churches.

(I qualify my "never" by "almost never," because he himself publicly announced a former error regarding a significant issue. Whereas he had once uncritically assumed the tradition that the "innocent party" in a divorce may remarry, he came to see that marriage is a lifelong bond, unbreakable even by fornication. There were a few other issues during his ministry in the Protestant Reformed Churches about which, if he was not wrong, the Churches did not follow his lead.)

Hoeksema was almost always right.

He was right very early in his ministry, in the Christian Reformed Church. He was right in the "flag controversy" during World War I, as even Christian Reformed historians now openly acknowledge. He was right in the "Bultema Case," regarding premillennial dispensationalism. He was right in the "Janssen Case," regarding higher criticism of the Bible, particularly the Old Testament. He was right in the "common grace" controversy, regarding a love of God in Jesus Christ that is wider and broader than election and regarding a spiritual union of the church and the anti-Christian world. The fruits of this doctrine in the Christian Reformed Church today are God's own vindication of Hoeksema's stand for truth and godliness in 1924.

He continued to be right in the prominent place God gave him in the Protestant Reformed Churches.

The outstanding instance was the warning he sounded against

a covenant doctrine of a (saving) grace of God to all baptized children, conditioned by the faith and obedience of the children, and the instruction he gave concerning the unconditional covenant of grace, when in the late 1940s and early 1950s the Protestant Reformed Churches stood at the crossroads. That he was right in his theology of the covenant of grace is being proved, and publicly demonstrated, today by the inevitable development of the doctrine of a conditional covenant in the heresy of the federal [covenant] vision, as also by the bold and widespread teaching that God loves all the baptized children, desiring their salvation, where the federal [covenant] vision may not be countenanced.

But Hoeksema's instruction concerning the covenant in the controversy of the late 1940s and early 1950s was only the outstanding instance of his being right. There were many other instances, which, though of lesser magnitude, were important for the well-being of the Protestant Reformed Churches. At synod, for example, Hoeksema did not speak often, or quickly. But when he spoke, the synod usually heeded his advice, because he was right.

He was invariably right, because he worked hard and long to prepare himself for the critique or deliberation; because he studied every issue thoroughly; because he had a deep and broad grasp of the Christian faith as confessed by the Reformed church, with regard both to principles and application; because he was widely read in all branches of theology; and because the Spirit of Christ raised him up to be a leader in the church of Christ, giving him special gifts of mind, will, and speech.

There have always been such leaders.

Luther was one. Calvin was another. There have been others of lesser stature and place. They were men who saw the issues rightly, explained them clearly, and spoke out boldly. Most importantly, they stood for truth and righteousness uncompromisingly and fought for Christ's cause without regard for the cost to themselves. God has used these men to preserve the church and to lead her deeper into the truth.

May God continue to raise up such men in the Protestant Reformed Churches and in other true churches of Christ!

Envied

For all their worth to the church, these men have never been appreciated by all. Their enemies have always reproached them as dictators and popes. In his "Life of Calvin," Theodore Beza observed that Calvin's enemies slandered the Genevan Reformer by charging that he was ambitious, even aspiring to a new pope-dom. Hoeksema suffered the same evil-speaking.

Even their own colleagues chafed under their leadership. Karl-stadt's break with Luther was doctrinal, but personal resentment over Luther's leadership in Wittenberg also played a part. On his deathbed, Calvin recorded his awareness that the ministers of the neighboring city of Bern, Calvin's colleagues in the Reformed ministry, "have always feared me more than they loved me. I want them to know that I died in the opinion that they feared, rather than loved, me."

Just as envy played a powerful role in Jewish officialdom's delivering of Jesus to Pilate (Mark 15:10), so it was a factor in the expelling of Hoeksema from the Christian Reformed Church in 1924 and in the opposition to Hoeksema by a majority of his colleagues in 1953. (This is not to suggest that there were no doctrinal issues, or that the doctrinal issues were not fundamental. I have established these truths earlier in this book.)

Prominent Christian Reformed theologians and ministers, some of whom Hoeksema had rescued in the "Janssen Case," turned on him (to his great surprise and grief), because already in those early days of his ministry he was a dominant figure. He was always prepared; he was always convincing; he was always right.

In the great internal controversy of the Protestant Reformed Churches in the late 1940s and early 1950s, colleagues resented Hoeksema's leadership in the denomination, and were determined to diminish it, if not to destroy it altogether. It was not Hoeksema, but his antagonist in the ministry of First Church, who famously said in the days leading up to the schism, "The issue is simply this, 'Who is going to be boss of First Church?'" What motivated Hoeksema's adversaries came out in the vicious attack on his person before the secular court, when they charged that he was determined to rule, and what he could not rule he ruined.

Who will deny that the men specially gifted by the Spirit as leaders in the church did not sometimes contribute to the resentment by their own sinful weaknesses? Even the sympathetic biographers and historians say the same things about them all—Luther, Calvin, Gomarus, Kuyper: strong-willed; outspoken; impatient of contradiction, particularly with regard to the confession of sound doctrine; sometimes fiery of speech. On his deathbed, Calvin confessed, yet once more to his colleagues in Geneva, his occasionally unruly temper.

But what folly, what disregard for the church of Christ, what ingratitude to God, to reject these men on this account!

Their sins are not to be excused. But those weaknesses did not disqualify these men for the position God gave them. It is not even unthinkable that it is exactly a nature prone to such weaknesses that is essential to the use God makes of such men in the church.

What have been the consequences of the rejection of these leaders for those who rejected them? Where have the would-be leaders led their followers?

What did the rejection of Jesus by the envious Jewish officials mean for the nation of Israel?

Where did Andreas Karlstadt lead his followers, having rejected God's Luther? Into the debacle of the Peasants' War, the madness of Munster, and scattering.

What were the consequences of the rejection of J. Gresham Machen for the Presbyterian Church in the USA?

The end of the Christian Reformed Church's rejection of Herman Hoeksema is now plain for all the world to see.

For the Good of the Church

When I was a boy, my father and uncles, committed members of the Protestant Reformed Churches and diligent observers of the church scene, all, over coffee on a Saturday morning would agree that one of the main problems with the Christian Reformed Church was that they did not have Herman Hoeksema as leader. I was not so sure in those days. I am sure today. Where would the Christian Reformed Church be today had it listened to Hoeksema's instruction and warning concerning being genuinely Reformed in the world and had it respected, rather than resented and rejected, his God-given position of leadership.

And what has happened to those former members of the Protestant Reformed Churches who followed the "boss of First Church" and others out of the Protestant Reformed Churches in 1953. Where are their children, grandchildren, and great grand-children? With rare exception, swallowed up in the Christian Reformed Church, which as I write is in the process of jettisoning the "Three Forms of Unity" as its binding creeds, and publicly, shamefully pleads for the approval of practicing sodomites in its fellowship in its magazine, *The Banner* (see the editorial in the March 2009 issue).

In 2021, the Christian Reformed Church is about to legitimize homosexual "marriage."

According to Romans 1, the ultimate depravity.

"Contra-natural" fruit of common grace.

The good news is that, regardless of resentment and rejection, the men God raised up as leaders *led*. Luther led. Calvin led. Gomarus led. Van Velzen led. Kuyper led. Machen led. Hoeksema led.

Christ saw to it.

For the good of the church.

In Richard Newhouse's mock-indignation at Hoeksema's "*peccavi*" was recognition of Hoeksema's leadership in the Protestant Reformed Churches.

It was recognition of Hoeksema's true greatness as a leader in Christ's church.

Hoeksema was always right.

Hoeksema's response to Newhouse was not only the personal magnanimity ("largeness of soul") of one who could bear easily what might be considered (but was not intended as) an insult. It was also the spontaneous response of a God-given leader in the church, towards the end of his life and work, who had learned to pay the price, from friend and foe alike, of faithfully carrying out the demanding task that Christ his Lord had thrust upon him.

For the sake of the church.

Chapter 9

SILENCE ON THE SCHISM

During my three years of seminary training under him, from 1960–1963, Herman Hoeksema never spoke of the great schism of 1953 in the Protestant Reformed Churches. Never, whether in class or during the breaks, did he refer to, much less excoriate, the ministers who were responsible for the schism.

Indeed, he never made much in class of the doctrinal issue that was at the heart of the schism. When the subject of the covenant came up in Dogmatics, he would give it its due, explaining it as God's bond of fellowship with the elect in Christ, established by an unconditional promise. I think now he was checking on my orthodoxy, or the level of my theological development, by assigning me Genesis 17:7 for practice preaching at some point in my seminary years. But he did not dwell on the subject of the covenant. He did not delve into the doctrinal differences concerning the covenant in the Reformed churches. And he never made the subject an occasion for raising the history of the controversy over the covenant in the Protestant Reformed Churches for some six stormy years.

I did not recognize this curious silence at the time. I wish I had. Then, I would have pressed the matter at every opportunity, asking about the doctrinal, church political, and personal aspects of the conflict. Especially would I have requested of my professor the fullest and most detailed explanation of his understanding of the reality of the covenant, from its source in the triune being of God to its perfection in the new world. I would have inquired exactly how he came to his covenant conception and where its origins lie in the Reformed tradition.

Only after I was in the ministry, and Hoeksema was gone, did it strike me that he had said virtually nothing about the struggle of 1953.

Hoeksema's silence about the schism of 1953 puzzles me.

I entered the seminary in the fall of 1960, a mere seven years after the split. In numbers both of pastors and of members, the churches were still suffering the devastating effects of the schism. The deep wounds of that fierce war between colleagues and fellow church members (one must not measure the severity of church conflict by the size of the church) had to have been still fresh in his soul.

One might have thought that the schism and its doctrinal cause would have dominated the instruction, in class and out of class. Instead, the schism was never mentioned.

It was as if, had Abraham Lincoln lived, an aspiring politician studied government, one on one, in 1872 with the then retired president of the United States, never to hear of the Civil War and only now and again to be reminded, albeit forcefully, that separation of a state from the Union is revolution.

I have wondered why—why the strange silence? Was the subject too painful for him? Or, was he weary of fighting that battle? Or, did he think that he had written volumes on the schism and its doctrinal component and that any seminarian worth his salt could read, or should have read, what he had to say on the pages of the *Standard Bearer*? Or, did he regard the schism as past history, which must not interfere with the task of giving a complete, well-rounded theological education in the present?

The Exception

There was one exception.

In October, 1960, the schismatic "Protestant Reformed Churches" held a special synod in order to consider returning to the Christian Reformed Church. Hoeksema wanted to know the discussion and decision of this synod. It was, of course, unthinkable that he himself would attend the synod. But he had an agent at hand—me. I was summarily delegated, on behalf of Herman Hoeksema, the *Standard Bearer*, and the Protestant Reformed Churches. Since seminary was in session and since I was the only student, seminary was canceled for the duration.

Hoeksema's report in the *Standard Bearer* of the decisions of the schismatic synod was based on my first-hand account and on the documents I managed to gather. Hoeksema referred to my reportorial role: "According to our reporter..."; "This I learned from the party that reported to me."[1]

When I dutifully reported on the proceedings of the synod of those who had in fact separated from the Protestant Reformed Churches, Hoeksema talked about the schism of 1953, and the ministers who had brought it about. His chief concern was whether any of the delegates and congregations indicated, finally, a willingness to return to the Protestant Reformed Churches (none did). His inquiries about the synod resembled David's asking the messenger about the safety of the young man Absalom.

The motion at the special synod of 1960 to return to the Christian Reformed Church, vigorously promoted by many delegates

---

1 Herman Hoeksema, "Fast Disintegration," *Standard Bearer* 37, no. 4, 5 (November 15, 1960; December 1, 1960): 76, 101.

(none more vociferous on behalf of returning than Rev. H. De Wolf, Hoeksema's former colleague in First Church of Grand Rapids), failed on a tie vote of eight to eight. It would pass overwhelmingly at the synod of 1961.

My attendance at the schismatic synod was an eye-opener, if not for Hoeksema, then for me. But Hoeksema also learned some things. Within the very short span of seven years, the churches of that synod were disintegrating, as one after another of the synodical delegates admitted. Speakers disclosed that some of the ministers had in mind to return to the Christian Reformed Church as soon as the split occurred in 1953, if not before, and that these ministers had been working actively in the churches to this end since that time. All the while these ministers had been claiming publicly that they and their churches were determined to be and remain Protestant Reformed.

It was evident also from the angry speeches of some of the elders that they and others of the membership of those churches had been betrayed by the ministers. Having led the people out of the Protestant Reformed Churches with firm assurances that their churches were, and would always be, Protestant Reformed doctrinally, these same ministers were now bent on delivering the people over to the theology and life of common grace in the Christian Reformed Church.

Debate at a Schismatic Synod

I took copious and scrupulously accurate notes of the speeches and church political proceedings at that long-ago synod. From my aging notebook, I quote some of the comments that were publicly uttered in the course of the deliberations of that synod of 1960.

A few months earlier, at their regular synod, the schismatic

"Protestant Reformed Churches" had decided that the three points of common grace adopted by the Christian Reformed Church in 1924 are not Pelagian and Arminian. They had also confessed their guilt over the years in charging the Christian Reformed Church with these sins. This decision really settled the issue whether they should return to the Christian Reformed Church, although residual resistance delayed the return for another year. Rev. J. Blankespoor was right when he argued, in favor of the return, "We have lost the basis of separate existence in denying the three points to be Arminian and Pelagian."

Especially Rev. H. De Wolf repeatedly held this decision before the house as the reason why there should be no objection to returning to the Christian Reformed Church: "We have already said that the three points are neither Arminian nor Pelagian." "Besides," De Wolf added, "If we do not return to the Christian Reformed Church, we will simply disintegrate."

Elder Vandenberg replied: "For thirty years we have been taught the corruption of the three points and have taught our children these things. Now we are to unite with the Christian Reformed Church without repenting from our former stand or remarking on what we said before."

Arguing for a speedy return, Rev. A. Cammenga described his denomination: "a little pee-wee church as we are."

Elder Vandenberg responded: "Is the question of my religion the question of whether we will be a small or a large group?"

Rev. J. De Jong, ardent advocate of dissolving into the Christian Reformed Church, had a way at the synod of bluntly expressing the reality of synod's miserable situation, which the other ministers tactfully or fearfully skirted. In his heavy Dutch brogue, De Jong announced, "Ja, Misterr Chairrman, I am a great friend of compromise." Later, he declared, "Ja, Misterr Chairrman, there is no middle ground between the Hoeksema group (sic!) and the Christian Reformed Church."

Proposing an odd ground for ecumenicity, Rev. J. Blankespoor pleaded for joining the Christian Reformed Church in order to work with likeminded "conservatives" in that denomination "to solve problems of corruption in the Christian Reformed Church." This strange ground for returning indicated how the "conservatives" in the Christian Reformed Church were wooing the separated "Protestant Reformed Churches." History has shown that the Spirit of genuine church unity was not overly impressed with this ground for union.

Rev. B. Kok was aggressive: "We sin against God and the Holy Spirit if we now do not join the Christian Reformed Church." Against an elder who had called the synod to honor the truth [of particular grace] in its debate and decision, Rev. Kok responded, "Unity is the truth too."

Rev. A. Petter, who had vigorously defended a conditional covenant during the controversy in the Protestant Reformed Churches leading up to the split of 1953, was adamantly opposed to returning to the Christian Reformed Church under the condition that he recognize the three points of common grace as biblical and confessional. "The three points of common grace adopted by the Christian Reformed Church in 1924," he insisted, "are not Scriptural and confessional." He added: "I will not stand by and let the Christian Reformed Church condemn Hoeksema, Danhof, and Ophoff again." Then he put a question to his colleagues who yearned to return to the Christian Reformed Church at once, "Can't our eager brothers show us, who have conscientious objection to the three points, some of the love they reveal to the Christian Reformed Church, by waiting for awhile?"

Petter weakened his case by many prodigiously long quotations from Reformed theologians on common grace. He noticeably wearied the synod, most of whom had no interest in the doctrinal issue.

In a characteristic comment, a mournful Rev. P. Vis lamented, "Years ago we were united on common grace, now even we, small as we are, are divided." A year later, at the synod of 1961, as the discussion moved inexorably towards the decision to return to the Christian Reformed Church, Rev. Vis would cry out, "Now I have to choose. The situation has arisen which I feared. I can neither vote for nor against this motion [to return to the Christian Reformed Church, acknowledging that the three points of common grace of 1924 are not Arminian and Pelagian and promising not to "agitate" against them]. I don't want to say that the three points are not contrary to scripture. Nor do I care to say that the three points are contrary to scripture. I don't want to carry on as a little group nor do I care to buck my conscience. I'm in a rough spot."

Rev. W. Hofman remarked, "Our association with the Christian Reformed Church in schools, institutions of mercy, and the like [over the past seven years] reveals to us that there is an essential unity between us." He added the warning that "ever since 1953 we as a church have been breaking down."

Rev. L. Doezema renounced the reformation of 1924 root and branch: "We should not have broken fellowship with the Christian Reformed Church because of the binding three points of 1924." Later in the debate, Rev. Doezema expressed the extent to which the theology of the "well-meant offer" had already developed in his thinking. Rev. Petter had raised the doctrinal issue of common grace. Petter had stated, "I and Rev. J. Howerzyl believe in one grace only; we cannot believe in two graces." Rev. Kok had responded, "I believe in conditions in the covenant and an offer of the gospel." Rev. Doezema then announced, "I believe in one grace—saving grace that is common to all humanity."

Rev. E. Knott, president of the synod, spoke against the motion to return to the Christian Reformed Church. "If I ever became a minister of the Christian Reformed Church [under the stipulations laid down by the Christian Reformed Church], I would never dare say another thing about common grace. Our entire historical position is essentially refuted by our entrance into the Christian Reformed Church under the present stipulations."

Exactly so! And the next year his denomination joined the Christian Reformed Church under these stipulations, himself included.

That the return to the Christian Reformed Church would shut the mouths of the returning preachers regarding criticism of the three points of common grace, and that the preachers understood this, came out in a sharp exchange between Rev. De Wolf and Rev. Howerzyl. The motion to return had already failed, much to Rev. De Wolf's disappointment. To Rev. Howerzyl, who had voted against the motion to return at that time, De Wolf put the question, "Do you actually intend to speak out [in the Christian Reformed Church] that you believe one grace and one grace only" [that is, that Howerzyl denied common grace]? Howerzyl replied, "Yes." De Wolf shot back: "You better not explicitly say such things in the Christian Reformed Church."

It was an especially poignant, and tense, moment when an elder in the consistory of the First Church of Rev. De Wolf, Van Tuinen by name, addressed the body (the synod had taken a decision allowing all elders in the denomination to speak, regardless that they were not delegates to synod). "Why are we in such a terrible situation? The preachers have been leading us in the way of the Christian Reformed Church. I would prefer to go back to 1953, when we left the Protestant Reformed Churches." Under pressure, the elder corrected himself: "when we left Rev. Hoeksema." He continued: "Then we said that we would be the continuation of the Protestant Reformed Churches. History has shown that they [the ministers in Van Tuinen's denomination] have set aside these arrangements and expected us [the people] to follow. We will not. I want to go back to 1953 when we left Rev. Hoeksema."

This same elder would speak out again at a session of the synod of the schismatic "Protestant Reformed Churches" in 1961, when those churches did decide to return to the Christian Reformed Church. Before a large audience of visitors, Van Tuinen exclaimed, in obvious distress, that "within six months of our leaving the Protestant Reformed Churches Rev. De Wolf was urging our young people to go back to the Christian Reformed Church. We elders had to reprimand him for this." This time when the president of the synod interrupted him to require that he substitute "the churches of Hoeksema" for his "the Protestant Reformed Churches," Van Tuinen defiantly repeated, "the Protestant Reformed Churches."

Decisions of a Schismatic Synod

When the motion to return to the Christian Reformed Church failed, the synod adopted a letter to the Christian Reformed Church asking that the three points of common grace be set aside as non-binding. Of all the foolish decisions ever taken by a Reformed synod, this one has to rank as among the silliest. In actuality, though not expressly, it was asking the Christian Reformed Church to repent of the grievous sin of adopting false doctrine and of the equally grievous sin of excommunicating and deposing faithful officebearers and people of God. It expected the Christian Reformed Church to go back on the theology of common grace, which has driven that church doctrinally and practically ever since 1924. It really politely requested the Christian Reformed Church to confess its wrongdoing to Herman Hoeksema and the true Protestant Reformed Churches, if not to seek reunion with these churches under stipulations laid down by the Protestant Reformed Churches.

The letter was foolish also because the schismatic "Protestant Reformed Churches" had to return to the Christian Reformed Church, regardless of the demands upon them by the Christian Reformed Church, and everyone knew it. The only alternative was returning to the Protestant Reformed Churches, and to a man the ministers of the schismatic churches opposed this. But in the meantime, as speaker after speaker at the synod of October, 1960 reminded each other, their denomination was "falling apart" and "dying." The always blunt Rev. De Jong exposed the foolishness of the letter to the Christian Reformed Church that the synod was in the process of adopting. "Ja, Misterr Chairrman, [we are saying to the Christian Reformed Church], 'Please remove the three points, but if you don't we will come across anyhow.'"

The Christian Reformed Church must have shaken its collective head in wonderment when it received the letter.

Needless to say, the Christian Reformed Church declined the request to set aside the three point of common grace as non-binding.

The Sad End of the Schism

The synod of the schismatic "Protestant Reformed Churches" met again in July, 1961, to consider the motion once again that had failed in October, 1960: return to the Christian Reformed Church. This time things went more smoothly. There was still resistance, especially from elders. A few ministers, with no heart for returning to the Christian Reformed Church, hopelessly bewailed their dilemma. All were forced to acknowledge that returning under the stipulations laid down by the Christian Reformed Church meant accepting the three points of common grace as biblical and Reformed, although in the finest political style of the Christian Reformed Church the judgment was couched negatively: not un-Reformed; not Pelagian and Arminian. All were reminded that joining the Christian Reformed Church meant that there would be no criticism of the three points of common grace.

On Thursday, July 13, 1961, at 2:36 in the afternoon, by a vote of eleven to five in a secret ballot, the synod decided to return to the Christian Reformed Church.

Thus was concluded for the schismatic churches a wicked piece of work. And thus was exposed the wickedness of their division of true churches of Christ before the world.

God meant it for good.

The Protestant Reformed Churches were tried as by fire concerning their love of the truth of the gospel of sovereign grace. They were purified especially of ministers whose hearts were not with the Protestant Reformed Churches in the unity of the love of the truth. And the doctrinal controversy, at the heart of the schism, established the Protestant Reformed Churches in the truth of sovereign grace with regard to the covenant. This doctrine is fundamental to the gospel. It is at the heart of the decisions of Dordt. It is thrust to the forefront today in all the reputedly conservative Reformed churches by the heresy of the federal [covenant] vision.

Silent about the Schism

But my interest in this book is Herman Hoeksema, as I knew him.

Within seven or eight short years after the split that climaxed six or seven years of violent controversy in the Protestant Reformed Churches, Hoeksema was vindicated. During the controversy, his name was blackened, his motives were impugned, his life's work was attacked, the congregations he had labored long and hard to build up were torn or destroyed, his own congregation was decimated, and he lost family and friends. Of particular, painful injury was the constant charge by the enemies that the issue was not doctrinal, but merely "personal" (the implication being always his evil person).

In the hasty, ignominious departure into the Christian Reformed Church of those who had separated from the Protestant Reformed Churches, the God of church history expressed a preliminary judgment on the schism of 1953.

One might have expected a long series of editorials in the *Standard Bearer* setting straight the record of the past thirteen or fourteen years. There was nothing of the sort. Two editorials on "Fast Disintegration" followed the abortive synod of October, 1960. One editorial on "A Sad End" informed the readers of the *Standard Bearer* of, well, the sad end of the schismatic churches.[2]

And during the three years of my seminary training, right at the time of his vindication, Hoeksema was almost completely silent about the great schism of 1953.

I think a great man of God was confident that, in time of crisis, he had fought a good fight on behalf of the truth and on behalf of the church of Christ. God had rendered His own resounding

---

2 Herman Hoeksema, "A Sad End," *Standard Bearer* 37, no. 20 (September 1, 1961): 460–461.

judgment on the schism in the history of the two denominations. The Protestant Reformed Churches had been preserved (though barely as it seemed to us). The clear, uncompromising testimony to particular, sovereign grace and to the antithesis was still maintained in the community of Reformed churches.

Do not dwell on the past, whether with bitterness, grief, or nostalgia. Press on to the things that lie ahead.

The spirit of a great man.

Chapter 10

VIGNETTES OF
A SEMINARY TRAINING

Vignette (vin-yet): "a short descriptive literary sketch;" "a brief incident or scene" (*Webster's Ninth New Collegiate Dictionary*).

Herman Hoeksema was an old man when I was in seminary (1960–1963). Born in 1886, he was seventy-four when I entered seminary and seventy-seven when I graduated. After my graduation, he had only two more years to live. Naturally enough, he had lost something, even a great deal, of the liveliness of the days of his great powers. He informed me once, after his criticism of my sermon at a practice preaching session, that he had "mellowed" over the years. (I breathed a silent, heartfelt prayer of thanks that I had been born opportunely.)

But he was still in possession of all his faculties, especially his theological and exegetical faculties, and he was still Herman Hoeksema.

One may have his own opinion about the merits or demerits of the ironclad law that is now in place retiring professors of theology at the Protestant Reformed Seminary at age seventy. But I bless

God that no such law was yet in place from 1960 to 1963, depriving me of studying under Herman Hoeksema.

Although I was the only student the first two years and one of only two students the last year, the classes were conducted as formally as though there were a student body of a hundred. Hoeksema lectured, sticking strictly to his subject and determined to cover all the material. There was no wasting of time, or implicit diminishing of the seminary, by idle conversation.

The Primacy of Exegesis

Mostly, the lectures consisted of his reading and commenting on his own published syllabi or printed outlines. Hoeksema had the fascinating habit of reading over a glaring grammatical error in his manuscript, which in those days, before copy machines, was printed in a primitive form, only to stop, suddenly, in his reading, in order to ponder the grammatical barbarity aloud. His tone of voice as he repeated the grammatical blunder was that of an inquisitor gravely evaluating some horrendous heresy. Invariably, he would shake his head sadly and conclude that the crime was that of some student copyist.

Of special benefit to me were the New Testament exegesis courses. The Rev. Herman Hoeksema, first and foremost a preacher of the word of God, was a brilliant exegete (interpreter of the Bible). Upon good exegesis, he never tired of reminding me, good preaching depends. Often, the worth of the dogmatics class was enhanced by his careful interpretation of a passage of scripture upon which the Reformed doctrine he was explaining was based. The format of the exegesis courses was that Hoeksema gave his exegesis of a passage in one class (which I wrote out word-for-word in my notebook). I read my exegesis of an assigned passage in the following class. Hoeksema would then critique my exegesis. The benefit of the course was especially the student's observance of Hoeksema's exegesis, not only the content of the passage, but also the way in which he went about interpreting it.

One year, he was working his way in class through the book of Philippians. I give a sample of his exegesis. Hoeksema worked with the Greek text and sprinkled his comments with the Greek words and phrases. In this sample, I use the corresponding English words and phrases. The text was Philippians 2:3: "Let nothing be done through strife or vainglory; but in lowliness of mind let each esteem other better than themselves."

The word "strife" originally was used to indicate those who ran for public office and courted popular applause by trickery and low arts. It comes from the verb meaning "to spin wool" as the attribute of a hireling. In the New Testament it has come to mean "a desire to put one's self forward," "a partisan and factious spirit which does not disdain low arts," "rivalry," and "ambition." Its close associate is "vainglory," "groundless self-esteem," "empty pride." In fact, ambition has its roots in vainglory. The latter is the basis of the former. Every man burns with esteem of his own worth. He values himself far above all others and thus would advance himself by any and all means to the forefront, where attention is his. And thus he envies the success of everyone else, strives with others in bitter jealousy, and rejoices at the failure and trouble of others. Such a condition among men, such concern for one's own advance, and such magnifying of one's own self simply are incompatible with love, sympathy, and likemindedness. Where true, spiritual love is, there will be found no factiousness and no vainglory. And it is, we notice, vainglory, glory that is mere illusion, empty pride, pride that has no content, thus no reason for being. If there were even a basis for that pride in self, it would be something. But there is no basis because all glory of man is like "the flower of the field" (Isa. 40:6). All the esteem of a man for himself is folly, for man is a depraved creature. Only one glory has worth, only one glory provides a basis upon which man can act and which can regulate all man's activities, and that glorying is the glorying in God. That alone is not "vainglory" but "real-glory" (here, Hoeksema did some word play with Greek terms, creating a Greek word meaning "full glory" to contrast with the Greek word translated "vainglory" in the text, which literally means "empty glory").

Exegesis serves preaching. Hoeksema was determined to give the churches good preachers and good preaching. One requirement for good preaching, he insisted, is that preachers preach series of sermons, and not jump around in the Bible from isolated text to isolated text. Series preaching is the Reformed tradition. But Hoeksema's reason for urging the preaching of series is intriguing. "Preaching series of sermons is preferable to random preaching," he said. "In this way the preacher can say 'Amen' conscientiously."

Fiery Debate

Prof. Herman Hoeksema welcomed questions from his student and the discussions that ensued. Questions often resulted in responses, which, though interesting, were not those that were expected. I asked him once about Erasmus' book, *The Praise of Folly*. I had just read the book and enjoyed the humanist's satirical attack on the Roman Catholic clergy. I expected a blistering condemnation of the Roman Catholic Church and, perhaps, some praise of Erasmus. Nothing of the sort. "Erasmus," Hoeksema replied, "I know him. But I don't like him. I don't like him because, although he knew that the Reformation was right, he remained in the corrupt Roman church. And this he did for his own convenience. Men like him, I have not much use for."

On one occasion, discussion turned a dogmatics class into a fiery debate. I was not involved. It was in December, 1961. The debate featured Hoeksema and the Rev. Prof. George M. Ophoff. Ophoff had retired in 1959. But he was still interested in theology. Twice a week, he would visit Hoeksema's dogmatics class—alert, discerning, enjoying, and, when necessary, participating.

In this particular class, Hoeksema was lecturing in Christology. The topic was the incarnation of the Son of God and the virgin birth. Concerned to safeguard the deity of Mary's child, as well as the sheer grace of the coming of the Son of God into the world, Hoeksema denied that Mary's part in the conception of Christ was the production of a "seed." This caught Ophoff's attention. Concerned to safeguard the true humanity of Mary's child, Ophoff insisted that something of the woman is "fructified" in the intercourse that results in conception. But Ophoff had the misfortune to call this "something" a "seed." This put Hoeksema instantly on his guard against transgressing scripture's teaching that the male was excluded in the conception of Jesus Christ.

Biological confusion having been firmly established from the outset, the battle was joined. For the entire hour, the exchange was hot and heavy. In frankest terms, the two theological giants, close colleagues, and old friends delved deeply into the physiological intimacies of conception. "Seed," "*sperma*" (so, reference was made to "sperm")," "*ovums*," "*zygotes*," and "*embryo*" flew back and forth across the classroom like so many bullets in warfare. Although I was the only student, for whose theological benefit, presumably, the debate was raging, I was as forgotten as though I had been on the moon. The debate became heated. Ophoff was excited, and not a little irritated. Finally, Hoeksema called a halt. "George, George, we should stop this."

The debate had its hilarious moments. I confess that at one point in the debate I could not refrain from laughing out loud (which went completely unnoticed).

But in the minds of the antagonists, the issues were doctrinal, and deadly serious: on the one hand, the Godhead of Jesus and grace; on the other hand, his genuine humanity. I did not miss this. Everything is theological, and sound theology is essential.

The tenacious Ophoff did not give up after one inconclusive battle. Hardly had we settled into our seats at the next class than Ophoff returned to the matter of "*sperma*" and "*ovums*" in regard to the conception of Christ. He had been thinking and studying. This time he carefully avoided calling the "something" Mary contributed to the conception of Jesus "seed." Ostensibly respecting his position as a guest and visitor in the class, he couched his carefully crafted argument as a question. But the question was, in fact, a long argument in favor of his position, concluding with the assertion that the Holy Spirit "took the place of the male organ" in the conception of Jesus and with the pointed question, whether the Spirit also supplied the ovary. Hoeksema did not rise to the bait. He declined to go into the matter any further, and headed off another heated debate, with the soothing words, "It is a mystery." And so it is. Ophoff yielded.

Spiritual descendants of those two men have doctrine— *sound* doctrine—(and controversy) in their bones.

Criticism in Practice Preaching

Hoeksema's criticism in practice preaching was incisive, helpful, and sometimes biting. He may have mellowed by my day, but he retained a tang. Criticizing my sermon on 1 Peter 1:3, Hoeksema remarked that my pauses were too long. "I wondered if you forgot your sermon." Concerning my delivery in delivering myself of a sermon on Isaiah 40:1–2, he said, "When you hold out your big hands, you spread your fingers. Shut your fingers." (I had not thought of this criticism for fifty-odd years, until I read it in an old notebook in preparation for writing this chapter. To my amusement, I am inclined to think that what I am told is a habitual gesture of mine—raising a hand with the fingers tightly closed—is the lasting, odd effect of Hoeksema's ancient advice.)

And then the criticism that is devastating, sending the seminarian home in a reflective mood. Critiquing my sermon on Isaiah 43:1–2, Hoeksema noted that "you had opportunity to speak about the cross, but never did."

Herman Hoeksema's criticism of my sermon on Proverbs 3:33 occasioned a delightful exchange between him and his son, Prof. Homer Hoeksema. Herman Hoeksema usually was the last critic. He had the final word. One of his criticisms of my sermon on the proverb was that it had only two points. (Proverbs lend themselves to two points to the inexpert and inexperienced preacher.) Herman Hoeksema proposed three points. Homer Hoeksema then did something unusual. With filial reverence and professional courtesy, he invariably deferred to his father. This time, he spoke up, coming to my defense (which endeared him to me). Addressing his father, he said, "You preached on this text once, and you had only two points." Herman Hoeksema considered this discrepancy for a moment, and then responded: "Well, when Dave has been a minister for forty years he also may preach it with only two points."

Hoeksema's instruction was not limited to the classroom, or to the subjects in the curriculum. He regarded all aspects of seminary training as properly his concern. He was teaching with a view to the lifelong ministry of his student. And he was observant.

Extra-Curricular Advice

Occasionally, I would speak a word of edification as a seminary student in the old First Church at the corner of Fuller and Franklin in Grand Rapids. This was daunting. Hoeksema would be prominently in the audience. The church was historic. Even the vast, impressive auditorium was intimidating to a seminarian. Late one Sunday afternoon, living away from my mother and as yet without a wife, I dressed for my appointment in First Church in an appropriate black suit and, without giving the matter any thought whatever, in a pair of white, athletic socks.

The next morning at the seminary, over coffee, Hoeksema matter-of-factly remarked, "Your sermon last night was good, but I would not wear white socks on the pulpit, if I were you."

Shortly after I began seminary, Hoeksema made it clear that he strongly disapproved of seminarians marrying while in school. "It detracts from their studies." During my last year, with a studied casualness that did not fool me, he indicated that he did not think it wise for a seminary graduate to take a charge unmarried. He spoke vaguely of the possibility of "talk."

Did he stop to consider that his program for the marriage of a seminary student gave the student a brief, four-month window to carry out the marital program—sometime between early June, when he graduated, and early October of the same year, when he would be ordained?

Did it enter his calculations that a young woman would necessarily be involved, who might have a program of her own?

And a mother-in-law?

Probably not.

His timetable was the best for the ministry and, therefore, should be followed. Furthermore, he had done it.

I could assure him that I would be married in the prescribed period. His hearty congratulations did not quite hide his relief.

Then there was the memorable last class of my last day at seminary. He did something he had never done before. He ignored the subject matter. But he did not engage in frivolous talk. He had important things to say at our parting. Among them were two exhortations, one carefully, but unsuccessfully, disguised, the other blunt.

"David," he said, "you will soon graduate and be eligible for a call in the churches. You will receive a number of calls." (There were many vacancies in those days, not long after the schism of 1953, and I was the only graduate.) "I must not advise you where to go, of course (of course, this was exactly what he was doing, and we both knew it), but I like Loveland [Colorado], and they have a great need. They are a new congregation, and they have been vacant quite awhile."

His advice was good.

And then this, as his last word, a kind of blessing:

When you become a minister in the Protestant Reformed Churches, do not preach dogmatics. Do not preach my dogmatics. (Picking up a Bible and holding it in his tremulous hand), preach the word. Preach the word. And if the churches put you out as a heretic for preaching the word, preach the word.

Ah, yes, I remember Herman Hoeksema.

Chapter 11

THE FINAL TEST

"That's all I have, Mr. Chairman..."

With these words to Rev. J. A. Heys, president of the synod, Rev. Herman Hoeksema leaned back in his seat, off to my left, in the front row of the delegates assembled as the 1963 synod of the Protestant Reformed Churches. Slowly he closed the black folder out of which he had been examining me in Dogmatics.

The place was the basement of the original building of First Protestant Reformed Church of Grand Rapids, Michigan, at the corner of Fuller and Franklin. In the auditorium of this church, as a small boy, some twenty years earlier, from high in the balcony I had caught my first glimpse of Rev. Hoeksema. For the past three years, I had been training for the ministry under him and Professor Homer C. Hoeksema in a small room across the hall from the large room in which synod was meeting, I was sitting, and the way into the ministry in the Protestant Reformed Churches would be opened to me.

I hoped.

The time was Friday morning, June 7, 1963.

No Relief

At these words, I permitted myself a small, concealed sigh of relief. Four and a half hours of examination remained. But I had made it, more or less successfully, through the part of the public examination before synod that consisted of questioning by Herman Hoeksema in Dogmatics. Dogmatics is by no means the only subject in the seminary curriculum, but it is the main one. The time allotted at synod for the examination of a seminarian in Dogmatics is far longer than the time devoted to any of the other subjects. And every graduate from the Protestant Reformed Seminary knows that he must do well in the Dogmatics examination. Dogmatics gives the aspiring minister of the word and sacraments the essential content of his preaching and teaching.

Towards the very end of the examination, I had stumbled. The question concerned the doctrine of the last things. Hoeksema had asked about the structure of the book of Revelation. The precise answer escaped me. All that came to mind was a vague statement of the intensifying conflict between the kingdom of the beast and the kingdom of the Lamb. Not content with this generality, and teaching to the very end, Hoeksema hinted broadly at the opening of the book by the Lamb in Revelation 5. Recovering myself, I made haste to say that I would like to "revise" my previous answer by referring to the opening of the seven seals, the sounding of the seven trumpets, and the pouring out of the seven vials.

"You must not 'revise' your previous answer," Hoeksema responded, genially, "but retract it."

I had stumbled, but the stumble was not fatal.

The exchange had even drawn a chuckle from the delegates, in which I fancied I could detect some slight sympathy.

A sense of relief at this juncture in the grueling proceedings was appropriate.

Three and a half hours of intensive grilling in Dogmatics by Herman Hoeksema were finished.

I sat alone on the raised platform—the only graduate of the Protestant Reformed Seminary. Before me was the august body of ministers, elders, and professors of theology in whose hands was my future—the "fathers of the synod," as Rev. Marinus Schipper was wont sonorously to address them in his pre-synodical sermons. They seemed eminently patriarchal to me on that June morning, some fifty-seven years ago now. They were not so much before me as I was before them. If I did not feel myself "naked to mine enemies," as Cardinal Wolsey once described his predicament on the way to his fateful meeting with King Henry VIII, I felt myself "naked to mine" dignified and powerful judges.

It was a very hot and very humid June late morning. If air conditioning had been invented, it had not yet been installed in the basement of First Church.

And I had troubled my already burdensome synodical examination by a foolish decision. The night before the examination would begin, I had yielded to the temptation to play ball. (In my defense, mitigating, though not excusing, my fault, the temptation was well-nigh irresistible. It was fast-pitch softball, and the game was an important one.)

My chastisement was swift and severe. It was inflicted by the powerful right arm of a young Harlow Kuiper. Throwing across the diamond as I wandered about the mound, preoccupied with an impending synodical examination, the youthful Mr. Kuiper (who had an arm, as they say, like a cannon) struck me with great force full on the bones above and below the left eye.

I preached my specimen sermon to the synod the next morning in the auditorium of the old First Church with my left eye completely closed and the flesh around it hideously multi-colored.

I gave my answers to the questions in Dogmatics glaring out upon the examiner and the "fathers of the synod" with one eye, and with the nagging thought, "What must they think of a seminary graduate who played ball the night before his synodical examination?"

Surely, I could afford to relax just a trifle at the conclusion of the all-important Dogmatics examination.

"…except that I have one more question for Mr. Engelsma," Hoeksema continued.

I came to full attention, instantly on high alert. There was no doubt in my mind that, whatever this "one more question" might be, coming as it did after the examination in Dogmatics had been completed, it would be unique, and very likely uniquely difficult for me.

To me: "What is more real, the eternal counsel of God, or history?" In the question, "real" meant "important."

Hoeksema's countenance was solemn.

The examination in Dogmatics was continuing. Indeed, it had climaxed. There could be no relief.

The Final Question

The members of the synod did not appreciate the final question. Neither did I. But our failures to appreciate the question were of a different kind. They did not know the reason for the question. No doubt, they were puzzled by it. I understood full well the reason for the question. But I did not like it, and heartily wished Hoeksema had not asked it.

Throughout the three years of my seminary training, Herman Hoeksema and I had carried on a running debate over this very question. He affirmed that the eternal counsel of God is "more real" than history. Early on, already in the first year, studying the first locus of Dogmatics, Theology, I had respectfully demurred.

I did not deny that the counsel is "real," or even that the counsel is the source and foundation of the reality of history. But I challenged the comparison, "*more* real." History, I contended, is as "real" as the counsel, because "Jesus Christ died in history." "*More* real" tends to diminish the reality of history and thus the historical cross of Christ.

It was an indication of the great theologian's magnanimity (largeness of spirit) that he never shut me up by imposing his towering stature upon me, a mere student. He took my position seriously. He discussed the issue, rather than to lecture me about his stand. This was characteristic of the man. If one disagreed with him, *on the basis of biblical, creedal, and reasonable grounds*, Hoeksema was willing to discuss and debate.

Which is not to suggest that he changed his view in the least. Heart and soul, he was convinced that the eternal counsel is "more real" than history.

I had completely forgotten our interesting, and sometimes lively, debate over the reality of the counsel and history, eternity and time.

Hoeksema had not.

A final dogmatical question.

Testing

I frankly confess that I considered giving the answer I supposed Hoeksema wanted. For all I knew, the right answer might be decisive regarding my entrance into the ministry. The words, "one more question, Mr. Chairman," deliberately spoken by one who did not speak idly at synod, rang in my ears. Might his reservations about my position be more serious than I thought? Had he decided to make an issue of our difference before the synod, as part—the *climactic* part—of the all-important examination in Dogmatics? At best, the answer expressing my convictions might very well lead to a debate in which I must certainly come off poorly. Was not the entire synod of the Protestant Reformed Churches, committed as the Protestant Reformed Churches are to the highest esteem of God's eternal counsel, expecting a seminary graduate to reply, unhesitatingly, "the eternal counsel"?

But, no.

If the synodical examination of a graduate of the Protestant Reformed Seminary before Christ's assembled church and, thus, before Christ himself, means anything at all, it means honesty. Precious as the ministry in the Protestant Reformed Churches is, and, therefore, highly desirable, it must be sought and entered in the way of pure truth, or not at all. Anything else is unworthy of the church's head.

Carefully, but truthfully, I answered: "I reject the comparison. The counsel of God is 'real.' So also is history 'real,' indeed, 'as real,' because Christ Jesus died in history. The cross of Christ is, and must be, historical. The crucified Christ makes history 'real.'"

For the first time in three and a half hours of examination in the grand truths of Reformed Dogmatics, a broad smile broke across the face of Herman Hoeksema.

"Mr. Chairman, I am satisfied," he said. And if Herman Hoeksema was satisfied, the synod was satisfied.

I had not known Herman Hoeksema as well as I thought I did.

I got to know him better on that June morning, long ago.

Any other answer than the one I gave that morning would have disappointed him, would have disappointed him greatly.

His final question in Dogmatics was far more than a final *question*.

It was a final *test* of his student.

I had passed.

Chapter 12

———

ONE LAST SERMON

I visited with the Rev. Herman Hoeksema for the last time late in the summer of 1964.

I called on him one more time in the summer of 1965. But by this time the earthly house of his tabernacle had so broken down that there could be no visit, only a call.

In the late summer of 1964, Hoeksema was in the hospital, having suffered a stroke that effectively put an end to his public ministry. He would die in September, 1965.

We visited in the hospital. I found him in a wheelchair in a hallway. We talked a little about his physical affliction. With obvious interest, he asked about the Loveland, Colorado congregation, whose call I had accepted the previous fall, about certain of the members whom he knew, and about my work.

It was just before I left, as I was about to read scripture and pray with him, that he opened up his heart.

We do this occasionally to each other, sometimes without intending to. There is a truth that is dear to our heart, and pressing on it. Suddenly, the circumstances are propitious. We express this truth to another. There is no mistaking the ultimate importance of what we are saying. There need be no tears, no noisy insistence that what is said is of great importance, no raising of the voice. The tone of voice, the look in the eyes, the tremor of speech, and then the truth itself give the other a rare glimpse into the depths of our heart, the deepest wellspring of our life with God.

"I don't think I will ever preach again," Hoeksema said from his wheelchair, "but if I do, I know what text I will preach."

He did not have to tell me the text.

I already knew it.

I am not clairvoyant.

The Last Sermon of Vos

But I had just come from the home of the Rev. Gerrit Vos, who was also convalescing. Gerrit Vos was one of the very first graduates of the Protestant Reformed Seminary after the forming of the Protestant Reformed Churches in 1924. He was among that small, select, noble band of ministers in the Protestant Reformed Churches who bore the burden and heat of the day.

Vos was an outstanding, moving preacher. He was also a lovely soul. To know him was to love him, as one may verify by asking the old members of Hudsonville Protestant Reformed Church, where Vos served as pastor for many years.

I came to know him during my three years in seminary. Twice a week for three years, Vos drove in to the seminary from Hudsonville to teach me Dutch. At the beginning of the first class, he matter-of-factly commended the instruction he was about to give: "I come from Sassenheim [the Netherlands], where the purest Dutch is spoken."

At the first class, he tossed a cigar to me across the table—a "rum-soaked Crooks." For three years, very much in the spirit of the proceedings of the Synod of Dordt, we smoked as we read and discussed the Dutch. He acknowledged that the Theological School Committee might take a dim view of this practice, but, he declared grandly, "I am president of the Theological School Committee, and I say, 'We smoke.'" We smoked.

Appointed to teach Dutch, which he did, Vos had other intentions as well. He announced that he would give me instruction also in pastoral aspects of the ministry. One of his earnest admonitions, bound upon me with some feeling, was, "Remember, you can lead sheep, but you cannot drive sheep." In the providence of God, some twenty-five years later I was put in the position to exhort this wise counsel upon seminarians for twenty years, never failing to credit Gerrit Vos.

Regularly a delegate to synod, Vos was absent from the synod of 1963, at which I was examined and declared a candidate for the ministry. Getting on in years by that time (he would retire in 1966), Vos was ill, unable to attend synod. But at the end of the line of delegates to synod, family, and friends congratulating me upon my successful endurance of the synodical examination I saw the white mane of Rev. Gerrit Vos. He had driven to First Church, Grand Rapids from his sick-bed in Hudsonville to congratulate me.

I have long forgotten what the delegates to synod, my family, and my friends said to me on that occasion, some fifty-seven years ago. But I remember Vos' words, as if he spoke them yesterday: "Davey, may the humility of Christ be yours." With that, and that only, he turned on his heel, and was gone.

Now in the late summer of 1964, Vos lay again on a sick-bed, in the little room of the old Hudsonville parsonage, just off the kitchen. He had gone through a serious illness, during which he had struggled spiritually. Satan had tempted him. God had tried him.

Vos was a different personality than Herman Hoeksema. Vos wore his heart on his sleeve. He described his physical affliction in graphic, earthy detail. With tears streaming down his cheeks, he exclaimed, "Oh, it was awful. I have been through hell. I felt that God would damn me. I cried out to Him, 'Go ahead! Damn me! I deserve it! But I will love You out of hell!'"

Noticeably brightening as he recited these last words, Vos went on, "And then I knew I was a saved child of God. No one talks like this who is not saved."

"I hope I can preach one more sermon in Hudsonville," the old preacher of the gospel and saint continued. "I want to preach the parable of the Pharisee and the publican."

Indeed, "God be merciful to me, the sinner."

The heart of Gerrit Vos.

The Last Sermon of Hoeksema

And now Herman Hoeksema likewise contemplated preaching yet one more sermon in his beloved First Church.

"…and if I do, I know what text I will preach."

Hoeksema did not wear his heart on his sleeve. Regardless of stroke, wheelchair, hospital, and the obvious end of his ministry and life, Hoeksema was perfectly calm, self-controlled, and deliberate. There were no tears, no candid revelation of spiritual wrestlings, no outbreak of emotions.

Only eyes reflecting eternal things and the tremor of voice that unmistakably signal the opening of one's heart.

"I will preach the parable of the Pharisee and the publican."

As I already knew.

The last sermon—the word of God of pure mercy in the cross of Jesus Christ to a guilty, depraved, wretched, and otherwise absolutely hopeless sinner.

This was the word Hoeksema proclaimed from the beginning of his long ministry.

This was the word he had defended in all his theological and ecclesiastical battles against attack on mercy—free, sovereign, discriminating mercy. For a conditional mercy, a universal, resistible mercy, a mercy for all, which is dependent in the last instance on the sinner, is no mercy. It is rather ground for the boast of the Pharisee: "God, I thank thee, that I am not as other men are, refusing to perform the condition of repentance, by which I, in contrast, distinguish myself from the others, make myself worthy of forgiveness (and of the cross, whence forgiveness flows) and make thy mercy effective."

Even the repentance of the sinner, the heartfelt, heart-broken plea for mercy—the plea of the publican—indeed, especially the repentance of the sinner (without which there can be no reception of the mercy of pardon), is no condition. Repentance too is mercy. It is mercy working irresistibly in the object of eternal mercy making a way for itself into the soul of the elect sinner.

The preaching of this word—the word of mercy of Luke 18:13—had drawn the young man Gerrit Vos to Herman Hoeksema in the earliest days of the reformation of 1924, as Vos himself told me.

This word is the heart, the very wellspring, of the Protestant Reformed Churches.

How Herman Hoeksema preached, taught, developed, and defended divine mercy as preacher, theologian, seminary professor, editor, and author!

But now this word of mercy was the word of salvation for Herman Hoeksema the sinner, at the end of his ministry and life. From his wheelchair, he looked back over a Christian life and glorious ministry in which, nevertheless, he had defiled all his works with sin, including his good works, indeed, his very best works. He knew this well. When I hinted once that seventy-five years of life and forty-seven years of church history-making, often tumultuous ministry, warranted an autobiography, he responded that he "would not like to do that because then I would have to relate unpleasant sins and motives. Fact is," he concluded, "I would not care to write my autobiography at all."

From the same wheelchair, he saw impending death, which would usher him (as it does us all) into judgment before God, whose righteousness is awesome.

"I will preach the parable of the Pharisee and the publican."

The last sermon.

The sermon he would leave with the people of God.

But also the sermon that would carry Herman Hoeksema through the judgment into everlasting bliss and glory.

A great man.

By Jesus' declaration, not mine.

For this too is the parable of the Pharisee and the publican: "He that humbleth himself shall be exalted."

www.ingramcontent.com/pod-product-compliance
Lightning Source LLC
Chambersburg PA
CBHW060949040426
42445CB00011B/1067